BIG IDEAS IN SOCIAL SCIENCE

T0344009

SAGE was founded in 1965 by Sara Miller McCune to support the dissemination of usable knowledge by publishing innovative and high-quality research and teaching content. Today, we publish over 900 journals, including those of more than 400 learned societies, more than 800 new books per year, and a growing range of library products including archives, data, case studies, reports, and video. SAGE remains majority-owned by our founder, and after Sara's lifetime will become owned by a charitable trust that secures our continued independence.

Los Angeles | London | New Delhi | Singapore | Washington DC

BIG IDEAS
IN SOCIAL
SCIENCE

DAVID EDMONDS &
NIGEL WARBURTON

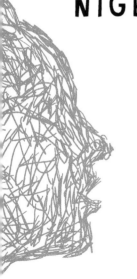

Los Angeles | London | New Delhi
Singapore | Washington DC

Los Angeles | London | New Delhi
Singapore | Washington DC

SAGE Publications Ltd
1 Oliver's Yard
55 City Road
London EC1Y 1SP

SAGE Publications Inc.
2455 Teller Road
Thousand Oaks, California 91320

SAGE Publications India Pvt Ltd
B 1/I 1 Mohan Cooperative Industrial Area
Mathura Road
New Delhi 110 044

SAGE Publications Asia-Pacific Pte Ltd
3 Church Street
#10-04 Samsung Hub
Singapore 049483

Editor: Kiren Shoman
Editorial assistant: Matt Oldfield
Production editor: Katherine Haw
Marketing manager: Michael Ainsley
Cover design: Wendy Scott
Typeset by: C&M Digitals (P) Ltd, Chennai, India

Library of Congress Control Number: 2015948264

British Library Cataloguing in Publication data

A catalogue record for this book is available from
the British Library

ISBN 978-1-4739-1379-0
ISBN 978-1-4739-1380-6 (pbk)

CONTENTS

ABOUT THE EDITORS

David Edmonds is an award-winning radio documentary maker for the BBC. He is the author and co-author (with John Eidinow) of several books, including *Wittgenstein's Poker* (short-listed for the Guardian First Book Award), *Bobby Fischer Goes To War* (long-listed for the Samuel Johnson Prize), and *Rousseau's Dog*. His most recent book is *Would You Kill The Fat Man?* He is a senior research associate at Oxford University's Uehiro Centre for Practical Ethics.

Nigel Warburton is a freelance philosopher, podcaster and writer, described by Julian Baggini as 'one of the most-read popular philosophers of our time'. His books include *A Little History of Philosophy*, *Philosophy: The Basics*, *Philosophy: The Classics*, *Thinking from A to Z*, *The Art Question*, and *Free Speech: A Very Short Introduction*.

The interviews for this book are based on a series of podcasts, *Social Science Bites*, sponsored by SAGE. *Social Science Bites* was inspired by the popular *Philosophy Bites* podcast (www.philosophybites.com), which was founded by David and Nigel in 2007, and has so far had 26 million downloads. *Philosophy Bites* has spawned three books, *Philosophy Bites*, *Philosophy Bites Back*, and *Philosophy Bites Again*.

FOREWORD

'Social science' is a broad and diverse grouping, what Ludwig Wittgenstein called a family resemblance term. There are many overlapping resemblances between the activities carried out under its name, but no uncontroversial defining essence. Social scientists include some of the most interesting intellectuals alive today, some in departments of sociology, psychology, anthropology, economics, political science, epidemiology, media and cultural studies, and elsewhere; others resolutely inter-disciplinary, or beyond academic pigeonholing altogether. As with any family, there are long-running disputes and rivalries as well as impressive collaborations and remarkable individuals. These disputes include differences about the nature and appropriate methodology of the social sciences. It is almost impossible simply to be a social scientist without reflecting on what you are doing and whether or not it is the right way to go about things. This makes any discussion about the nature of social science both interesting and inconclusive. It is easier, and perhaps more enlightening, to examine a range of social scientists' work, and to discuss how they understand what they are doing. This is what we have attempted in this book.

The book is a by-product of a podcast series. In 2012, we were approached by SAGE to conduct a series of interviews with leading social scientists. For some years we had already been running *Philosophy Bites* (www.philosophybites.com), interviewing philosophers about specific topics, and the idea was to do for social science what we had done for philosophy – make available, free of charge, globally, significant research by significant figures, in an accessible audio format. The result was *Social Science Bites* (www.socialsciencebites.com) and we have already been fortunate to record interviews with many of the leading social scientists of the 21st century.

For this book, rather than simply present verbatim transcripts, in collaboration with the interviewees we have edited what they said in order to make the interviews work on the page, while keeping the spirit of conversation. Some interviewees made minor amendments; others took the opportunity to suggest more significant revisions.

We would like to thank the sponsors of the podcast, SAGE, and especially Ziyad Marar. *Social Science Bites* is Ziyad's brainchild. He has been a pleasure to work with, combining a can-do attitude with relentless enthusiasm and intellectual curiosity, while allowing us extensive editorial freedom. We would also like to thank the rest of the team at SAGE, especially Katie Baker, Mithu Lucraft, Matthew Oldfield, Kiren Shoman, Katherine Haw and Michael Todd. Thanks also to Charles Styles, Hannah Warburton, and Mollie Williamson for transcribing interviews, and to Hannah Edmonds for proofreading the book.

For us, *Social Science Bites* has been both an adventure and a privilege. We've met many inspirational thinkers, who've been happy to spare time talking to us about their invariably fascinating research. We are extremely grateful to all of them; their enthusiasm for their research has been contagious.

Social Science Bites is ongoing. The interviews can be found here – www.socialsciencebites.

This book is dedicated to Ralph Oppenheimer.

David Edmonds

Nigel Warburton

June 2015

SECTION I

FIELDS OF ENQUIRY

1

ROM HARRÉ ON WHAT iS SOCiAL SCiENCE

Rom Harré was for many years the University Lecturer in Philosophy of Science at the University of Oxford. Moving from the philosophy of the physical sciences in the mid-seventies, he began a long series of studies of the metaphysics and related methods of research in the human sciences. He has been much involved in the

Spanish world, including South America. Currently he is a member of the Psychology Department of Georgetown University, Washington DC.

David Edmonds:	*Before setting out on a series of interviews on the social sciences, some rather fundamental questions need addressing. What is social science? How do the social sciences differ from the so-called 'hard' sciences, like physics and chemistry? Can social science be held to the same standards of rigour as 'hard' science and can we expect it to be predictive, and falsifiable? Who better to answer these questions than polymath Rom Harré, a distinguished philosopher, psychologist, and social scientist?*
Nigel Warburton:	*The topic we're focusing on is 'What is social science?'. Could you give a broad definition of social science?*
Rom Harré:	It's pretty hard to do that, but we could start with the idea that everybody lives in a society. That is, they live in families, in towns, in nations, and, of course, they want to know what it is they're living in. And suddenly, around two millennia ago, someone, namely Aristotle, thought to himself, 'Let's look at

this world that we live in.' It's a bit like fish discovering the sea. We live in a society, and suddenly we can start to ask ourselves, what is it and how does it work?

NW: *But that, in a way, is the kind of question that some historians might ask themselves: 'what is the nature of our world in relation to the way it has been?' But most people don't think of history, straightforwardly, as social science.*

RH: Well, over the centuries, sociology and economics have come to be the study of contemporary society. There is, of course, historical sociology where we ask ourselves what society was like in, say, the Middle Ages or medieval Japan. Gradually these two aspects have come closer and closer together. In the kind of work I do, I wouldn't dream of attempting to study a contemporary phenomenon without studying its historical antecedents. Years ago, my students and I did a study of football hooliganism and when we were working out the theory behind this, we thought, let's look in the past and see when similar things happened: apprentice riots in London, the battles between the supporters of the different horse-racing teams in ancient Rome – it's happened before. So sociology opens up into the past, and of course some people think it should also open up into the future.

NW: *So social science has a link to the past and you've said it involves focusing on social relations. It's also got the sense of being a science; how do you see the relationship between the social sciences and the natural sciences?*

RH: Both are in the same kind of enterprise; that is, they're trying to give us a picture of how things are in some domain of the universe. The difference is the social sciences are concerned with something we make ourselves: we create societies, but of course we don't create the solar system; we don't create the particles we study in the Hadron Collider. But in sociology we're looking at our own work, our own artefact.

NW: *So does that produce special problems in terms of achieving an impersonal stance or repeatable experiments?*

RH: There's one enormously important problem in dealing with sociology and social sciences generally. Because we create these social objects, we have to ask ourselves what's the instrument with which we create them? In the last 50 or 60 years, language has come to be seen as the key element in all of this. Now, once again another aspect of the human sciences, particularly linguistics – sociolinguistics, psycholinguistics – gets into the story. You can't draw a sharp separation. For example, if you want to understand the sociology of life in France, you'd better understand the grammatical difference between 'tu' and 'vous'.

NW: *That's intriguing. Obviously language isn't the only means of cultural transmission, so there must be many other ways into the social sciences.*

RH: There are lots; some of these are so small scale we don't even notice them: terms of address, costume, hairstyles, flags, monuments. If anybody wants to say anything important in the United States, like Martin Luther King, they go to the Lincoln Memorial, a gigantic chunk of marble, at the end of the Mall. There it is, America personified. So there are all kinds of carriers of social reality.

NW: *Let's return to the science question. How do the social sciences relate to other sciences?*

RH: It's first of all a matter of method. By and large social scientists and natural scientists are in the same game. They're trying to find, or develop, a system of classification: the sort of categories that you need to identify what it is that you're studying. Then you need to try to develop an explanatory theory, how it comes about that things happen the way that they do. In the natural sciences, you build working models, either in the laboratory or in your head, as to how the world works. In social sciences you try to do the same thing. However, you are part of the operation. Suppose you're making a working model of some aspect of social life, say family life, or say diagnostic activities in a clinic, that in itself is a piece of social life. The first thing you have to learn is the art of stepping back – well, stepping forward and stepping back. You have to be a participant observer in one way – to have a sense of what's going on. But you have to step back and pretend you're not part of that reality, to take a bird's eye view of it. This is why it's so important to think back to Aristotle, who was the first to step back and study the constitutions of the Greek states. But he was a member of a Greek state and he was seeing it within his own frame of reference, and of course within his own language.

One further point: English is the language of sociology. It used to be German, then it was French. Now it's English. I go to lots of countries. Everywhere I go, except South America, English is the *lingua franca* of the academic world. The social force of English is becoming part of the topic of sociology.

NW: *When we look back at the social scientists of the 19th century, we can easily see their biases: they have the assumptions of imperialism, for example. In the present it's quite difficult to be aware of our own biases. How would a social scientist go about eliminating, or allowing for, those sorts of prejudices?*

RH: I think we're aware that those prejudices exist. So one of the things you start training undergraduates, when they're doing a course in this kind of thing, is to get them to have a sense of their own world. I'm just about to set off to the States to teach a course in qualitative psychology, which is largely concerned with social matters, and the first exercise we're going to have is standing back; they will ask themselves what is it to be a member of Georgetown University, particularly those who support the basketball team? They should not take it for granted that they already know this explicitly. Much of sociological research is making explicit what we know implicitly.

NW: *With the natural sciences we often have the possibility of repeating experiments, manipulating variables, so we can get very accurate information about what's going on. If you were investigating an outburst of violence at a particular football match, you couldn't just go back and tweak the variables. So what does a social scientist do in that sort of situation?*

RH: There's a long-running controversy about whether the experimental method has any place at all in the social world. I'm one of those who are very suspicious of the attempt to hammer social life into shape in a laboratory, with three or four people trying to replicate the social behaviour of millions. I think it's a huge mistake. The issue then is how to produce useful, valuable material that's not just vignettes of the passing scene. You're trying to slide upwards a little bit towards some sort of level of generality. The way that people act in families is enormously different all over the world, but there are going to be certain sorts of commonality. The great mistake in the past, I think, particularly in social psychology, was to presume that you knew what the commonalities were, and then you could simply go around and see how many cultures exemplified them. Take the nuclear family. Well, if you go to New Guinea or Zimbabwe, there isn't anything very much like the nuclear family. In some societies all the boys leave Mum when they're nine or so, and go to live with dad, and they may not have much to do with Mum again for years and years. Something similar occurred in the English-speaking world with the public school institutions. It's a very different sort of life from other schools and tends to produce a different sort of person, I believe. So we have to be very cautious about the extent to which we generalise.

NW: *There's obviously a certain amount of descriptive work done in the social sciences, but it's often meant to be predictive of how people will behave, not just accounting for how they have behaved. How do you make that move from the past to the future?*

RH: It's extremely problematic and, notoriously, social scientists, economists, are very bad at doing this, because the amount of variation of human society is simply enormous. Things happen when we haven't got the faintest expectation that they will. For example, who would have imagined the last seven or eight years of chaos in the banking system? How is it possible for intelligent people to do the things they did? There they were, highly educated, well-established, brilliant people, with all the technology in the world, and they were taken by surprise. Who could have guessed that the Islamic Spring would turn so violent and chaotic?

NW: *So what is the value of social science research?*

RH: Well, I think it does give you a grasp of the world as it is at this moment, or rather as it was a little while ago. And that's not a bad thing: those who know no history are doomed to repeat it. But there's no guarantee that that knowledge is going to function like Newton's laws of motion. There is a kind of intuition that really brilliant social analysts or brilliant politicians have, in which they're drawing on millions and millions of tiny pieces of data, organising them somehow, coming up with a sense of what's going to happen.

NW: *There's been a huge change in the sources for social scientists with the internet, and with statistics and data being made free online. How is that changing the nature of the social sciences?*

RH: I think it may have a profound effect on sociology. This huge amount of data has led to a kind of despair. And we might find ourselves going back more often to micro-studies again, looking at how small groups of people function.

NW: *It strikes me that the best social scientists are also very skilful narrators: they know not just what's going on but they can tell the story in interesting ways to reach a wider public.*

RH: Well, yes, the great sociologists can tell stories. In fact, it's another aspect of contemporary sociology: the idea of narratology, looking at the way in which people can build their lives around story lines. One of the most recent specialties is called positioning theory: the sociologist studies the way people assign rights and duties to each other in terms of the stories that they persuade each other to believe and tell. For instance, you might think about a family quarrel in terms of the story of that particular family, how Mum and Dad came to meet, what's the history of their ancestry, the sort of things you see on the television, with people going back to find a family story. And of course that story is going to feed into a family itself and transform it. Discovering your ancestors is a way of changing the lives of your successors, because now there's a whole new story to tell.

NW: *Given the social sciences aren't always great predictors of what's going to happen, how can you tell good sociology, good social science, from bad?*

RH: Again that's very difficult to do. There's very little place for the methods you would use in the natural sciences. One way that has been talked about quite a bit over the last 20 or 30 years is bringing the research findings back to the people you are investigating and asking them 'Does this illuminate your life?'

It's kind of psychiatry on a large scale, where you bring the story back to the person who came to you with anxiety or suffering of some kind, and the person becomes convinced that this was so, and perhaps achieves some sort of relief. It doesn't matter whether the story is true or not: it's a matter of making sense of things. Years ago a group of us began to ask this question about plays. Are plays sociology? A very well-known sociologist, the late Stanford Lyman, thought they were, and he devoted quite a lot of time to studying the plays of Shakespeare, seeing Shakespeare as a sociologist. His idea was that the people of the time found Shakespeare convincing because he was telling stories that they recognised as the stories of their lives. So the way Hamlet and Ophelia behave is something that they recognised. So that's one way in which we can tell good sociology from bad. If you don't recognise it as part of your life, or the life of people you know, it's not likely to be convincing.

NW: *Social science is often thought of as including most anthropology, a lot of psychology, economics, sociology. Is there anything common to all these different enterprises?*

RH: The one thing there is in common is their attempts to understand a group of people and how they behave. Human societies are very complex, and there are many different aspects to their behaviour. We've said nothing about medicine, and about, for example, epidemics. Epidemics are a phenomenon in biology, but they have profound social consequences. A chemical discovery will transform the lives of millions of people socially. We now have ways of keeping people alive much longer than before: that's the result of medicine, a bit of biology – but with profound social consequences. So the one item that is in common to all these disciplines is the social world. Linguistics, history, economics, anthropology, geography, even geology are all part of sociology in a sense. The object of study is the same, but the methods of study are vastly different.

NW: *From outside the social sciences, there is often the prejudice that social scientists tend to be relativists. Whereas natural scientists think, on the whole, that they are discovering something about the way the world is, social scientists are prone to say 'Well, there are many different ways of describing the world, there's no one God's-eye view that we can discover.'*

RH: Well, certainly, half a century ago, the natural scientists were
              gung-ho, going for the truth, and it didn't matter where you
              did it, or who you were, or which laboratory you worked in;
              you were 'on the road to the truth'. But in sociology it
              gradually became clear that the societies you were looking
              at were very different from one another. What counted as a
              good marriage in Namibia wouldn't count as a good mar-
              riage in New York. So the idea that there were societies so
              different that each one had to be tackled separately was an
              important insight.

              But suddenly, about 40 to 50 years ago, natural sciences began
              to ask themselves the question: 'If I'd been brought up in a
              different way and worked in a different laboratory with a different
              set of instruments with different assistants helping me, would I
              have come up with the same answer?' What we're getting in the
              natural sciences is a series of snapshots around a common
              core – which is the world out there. In the physical sciences I'm
              notorious as a philosophical realist: I think we're studying reality.
              But we're taking shots from different points of view. That's not
              true in the social sciences because there isn't a world out there:
              there are any number of different practices that people are
              engaged in. It's not that there's a series of snapshots; the snap-
              shots *are* the object of enterprise. As I said at the beginning, the
              social world is a world we create, and in studying it we're con-
              tinuing to recreate it. Karl Marx sat in the British Museum
              studying British industrial society: of course what he then wrote
              down in *Das Kapital* became an instrument for the transformation
              of society itself.

FURTHER READING

Jerome S. Bruner, *Acts of Meaning* (Harvard University Press,1994)
Rom Harré and Paul F. Secord, *The Explanation of Social Behaviour*
     (Blackwell, 1973)
Rom Harré and Luk van Langenhove, *Positioning Theory* (Blackwell, 1999)

2

TOBY MILLER ON CULTURAL STUDIES

Toby Miller is Emeritus Distinguished Professor, University of California, Riverside; Sir Walter Murdoch Professor of Cultural Policy Studies, Murdoch University (40%); Professor Invitado, Escuela de Communicación Social, Universidad del Norte (25%); Professor of Journalism, Media, and Cultural Studies, Cardiff University/Prifysgol Caerdydd (20%); and Director of the Institute of Media, and Creative Industries, Loughborough University in London (20%). He can be contacted at tobym69@icloud.com and his adventures scrutinised at www.tobymiller.org.

Photo: Alys Tomlinson (http://www.alystomlinson.co.uk/)

David Edmonds: *Literature, physics, history, now these are proper areas of academic discipline. But cultural studies? Even compared to the other social sciences, cultural studies has attracted – from usually ignorant sources – particular derision. Toby Miller is a leading academic in cultural studies whose writings cover an astounding range of topics from TV and Hollywood to sport and the media.*

Nigel Warburton: *The topic we're focusing on is cultural studies. Could you begin by saying something about what you do, and why that's cultural studies?*

Toby Miller: Sure. I think the answer to the question 'What is cultural studies?' is ongoing and depends on the time and place that it's answered, although the same thing could be said about lots of disciplines as they merge through time, warp and woof, and interact with others. In my case I try to look at two particular factors in the everyday life of culture. The first is subjectivity, by which I mean not just 'This is simply my opinion', but rather how subjects are made, how persons are constructed, how positions are generated for them and how they occupy those positions – whether that's something the census says about you, or your mother says about you, or your religious affiliation says about you. Secondly, power: how those subjects are constructed in terms of different power dynamics, hierarchies, and opportunities for difference and contestation.

NW: *This idea of the relationship between the self and society sounds like sociology to me.*

TM: It's true that I'm a lapsed sociologist! But because my career's been split between Australia, the US, the UK and Latin America, I'm prone to different kinds of sociology. The one that most appeals to me is probably the more qualtoid, politically inflected, culturalist form you get in Latin America, and less the 'rats and stats' *quantoid* form that predominates in the United States.

NW: *Could you give an example of something that is cultural studies? What makes it 'cultural'?*

TM: By 'culture' most of us in the field would mean two things. First of all, what's often thought of as an aesthetic inheritance or an aesthetic heritage, namely the world of arts, the world of meaning, the world of textuality, the world of content. The way in which artists, authors, writers, radio producers generate things of beauty, things of truth, if you like – what we understand by 'the arts' or 'the humanities'.

Secondly there is an understanding of culture which is more ethnographic, perhaps more anthropological. This is about customary ways of life: the understanding that society is authored not only through formal rules and regulations but informal ones – the way in which we organise our daily routines, the way in which you and I are taking turns – politely, so far – with each other's sentences. And in cultural studies those things merge. In order to understand how art works, you need to understand everyday life, and in order to understand everyday life, you have to understand how art works. And that's especially true in many of the de-industrialising, post-industrialised societies like the UK and the US. Increasingly in these places, services, culture, ideas, meanings, insurance, law, and the media are being sold, not farming, manufacturing, or mining.

To give an example, do you like Hollywood, Nigel? What do you think about the Hollywood industry as a consumer, as a viewer?

NW: *I tend to go a bit more for the independent films… there are some great Hollywood movies, for sure.*

TM: This is the edgy, arty side of Nigel Warburton exposed to his multinational public. Well, in the books *Global Hollywood* and *Global Hollywood 2* that I wrote with a number of collaborators with Indian, Chinese, Spanish and US backgrounds, we tried to understand the success of Hollywood as a film industry around the world in many different contexts, but always trying to bear in mind three factors.

First, the underpinning political economy – in other words who benefits from all of this? How does the money move? Is the success of Hollywood not just about the supposed quality of what it produces, but its capacity to get hold of things like free money? In other words, not loans and not equity, but lunatic governments throwing money at it because they think Hollywood will produce glamour, tourism, or whatever. The UK is lunatic about that, Australia is, Hungary is – you name it.

A second aspect of all this, of course, is the meaning of these things. How is the success of Hollywood achieved through sights, sounds, narratives, and dramatic arcs? What are the special effects that generate the meanings that stand for Hollywood when you and I use the term?

And, thirdly, how are these things actually interpreted? What do we know about how audiences make meanings themselves as recipients of Hollywood?

So in other words, the way I do cultural studies is to examine ownership, control, regulation and so on; the meaning that's generated; and the experience of that meaning as it is in turn regenerated by audiences or spectators.

NW: *It strikes me that there are two distinct things going on: you're collecting empirical data about Hollywood, and presumably that's reasonably objective, but you are also spinning a story about Hollywood and that surely has a subjective element. How do you know that the story that you're spinning about Hollywood is a plausible story?*

TM: That's a really good question, because Hollywood in particular is one of these places where vast amounts of data are available. And one can deem them to be real and credible. But frankly they encourage words that one can't say on *Social Science Bites* but are running through our minds even as we speak. So when you go to sources like the major trade magazines, or the studios themselves, it's likely that you'll be told stories about, say, the success of *Skyfall*, a big James Bond movie – it cost this amount of money; it's taken in this amount of money; it will go through the following 'windows of release' that will generate the following revenue – and these stories are frequently fabricated. The only way you'll ever find out the *real* data is when there's a big law case and the books are opened in court. But, yes, we try to use lots of so-called 'hard' data that are about where the money goes. Some of that's reliable and some of it isn't.

However, to get to your question about how I spin the story, how I know that my story is legitimate, that's a very reasonable point. I'm a polemical writer, and I want to tell stories that appeal, firstly, to other scholars and so will meet the standards of rigour that are expected within the various disciplines that are germane to the topic I'm interested in; secondly, to stakeholders who will actually pay some heed to what I write; and thirdly, to the general public. Some people, when they read my academic prose, say 'Extraordinary empirical data – it's a pity this person is so biased.'

NW: *But you don't think it's biased?*

TM: No, I don't. My personal, political, intellectual commitments are very important to the work I do, but they don't structure or inform it in a totalising way. My overall commitment is to try to find out the nature of things and how they operate. That often means unveiling things that are very uncomfortable in terms of my political commitments. More generally, it means disclosing things that are uncomfortable for other people's political commitments. So, for example, most people think Hollywood is a truly laissez-faire private-enterprise industry, an example of the grandeur of American capitalism, the capacity to simply let entrepreneurs have their head without state intervention. That's simply not true. I've disproved it, as have many other people, hundreds of times. But there are plenty of people who say 'You're a socialist, that's what you're looking for; you don't understand that that's really irrelevant.' But my politics do not override the empirical material that I uncover.

NW: *How can you be sure of that?*

TM: Well, I get my work read by others who do not share my commitments. And I write so often and so much, but generally with time to spare, that I can go back and cast a critical gaze over what I've done. In terms of the Hollywood material, one of the interesting things to me is that I know producers, studio executives and Hollywood attorneys, who read the book and introduce me to others and say 'This is Toby Miller; he's a professor at the University of California (which I was). He's a socialist, but he actually understands how we go about what we do.'

That would be one case where I'm making a point about the hidden subsidies that characterise much of US capitalism: it's informed by what I suspect I'll find, as a consequence both of my social science background and my political commitments. And then when I find it, I have a diagnosis that I think is perfectly legitimate. But you don't have to accept the diagnosis in order to recognise that I am correct in the empirical material that I present.

NW: *Have you ever had the experience of taking your interpretation of events, or of an institution, back to the people who know it intimately and have them saying 'That's not us, it's nothing like us'?*

TM: Yes, I have. And frequently that's been an interesting lesson in and of itself. Whilst it's the case that a number of people working in Hollywood have found my analysis of their success and how they go about it very compelling, others have completely refused to engage or have denounced it, because, in my view, the reality of the degree of state participation in the success of this apparently laissez-faire industry is tough for them to hear. That doesn't mean their story, their version of these things, is worthless. I want to make sure that the voices that disagree with me are given plenty of space in what I write.

NW: *When I interviewed the psychologist Jonathan Haidt for* Social
Science Bites, *he told me how he'd moved from having strong
Democratic convictions more towards Republicanism, as a result of
his research. Is there anything similar you could envisage happening
to you?*

TM: My view is constantly changed by what I unearth and what I
encounter and what people tell me. An instance of that would
be my work for the book *Sportsex*, about sport and sexuality.
As part of my commitment to try to reach out to scholars, to
stakeholders, to the general public, I wrote newspaper op-eds,
and a couple of pieces in fashion outlets and gay websites, at
their request. One of those pieces was then reappropriated
by another website and illustrated with hardcore porn, without my being told, without the earlier gay website being told,
and with no name responsible on the website other than,
apparently, mine.

What was I to do with this? What was it telling me? There are
ethical and legal issues, but put those to one side. I learnt
from the episode that my writing in *Sportsex*, which was an
attempt to talk about the beauty of the male body as a grand,
new, vibrant commodity in the media, sport, and the public life
of bodies, was amenable to this profoundly erotic/pornographic
interpretation. So here I was finding my words illustrated,
without my say-so, by images that many people would find
deeply offensive – and yet there are some readers out there
for whom this connection was quite significant. So it was a
very interesting lesson in what can happen when you put
your foot into the water, in a certain domain, when suddenly
information can come back to you that's at variance with
what you were anticipating.

NW: *I was intrigued when you said earlier that your role is to disclose
'the nature of things'. Because the caricature of people in cultural
studies is that they don't think there is a nature of things: everything is constructed, there's always another perspective. But you
seem to be embracing an Enlightenment view of our relationship
to the external world.*

TM: Caught out! I thought that one was going over the boundary,
but I got caught in the deep. My answer to that would be to
turn to Bruno Latour – one of the great French anthropologists/

philosophers/sociologists of science. When Latour is asked about the nature of science, the nature of things, and the nature of meaning, he says you have to have all three in dynamic intercourse (as the actress said to the bishop).

So let me give you an example of what I mean, what Latour means, and how that informs my understanding. Yes, there are all kinds of different natures of things: things evolve and the struggles over what they are and how to deal with them evolve, and the struggle over how to represent them evolves, but all those three things need to be understood if you're going to get to the nature of things.

Latour has an example. Suppose you're a scientist and you are writing an article about a particular thing that exists in the natural world – let's say wind. On the one hand there *is* a thing called 'wind'; nobody in cultural studies is going to say that the flag is not blowing when the flag is blowing. But the decision to write about the flag, and the funding that comes to you to do so, will involve social forces, power relations, government decisions, financial investments, and so on. And the way in which you write about the wind will be informed by the rules of how to write a journal article: there will be an abstract, keywords, a method; there will be a literature search; and there will be a hypothesis. None of these things has anything to do with wind: it's to do with a set of forces, and to do with texts. So to understand the nature of things, you need to have all those things in dynamic play.

NW: *But when it comes to the interpretation of the significance of things, there's much more scope for debate than there is about the hard empirical data.*

TM: Yes, but deciding what to count and how to count it is incredibly important. Justin Lewis, a wonderful British scholar, wrote a great book on public opinion about a decade ago. Justin's point there, is that basically what happens with a lot of numerical sociology and communication studies is that there's a problem that exists which you can describe with words. We're talking on the day of the US presidential election: who is going to win between President Obama and Governor Romney? That will be decided empirically by numbers, but it is being constructed as a problem verbally. Once you've got that verbal problem, what it is that you want to know about, you then seek to turn the different categories that you've described into numbers: X number of people are doing this, Y number of people are doing that. Once you've done that and you go through the various numerical manipulations required of, say, mathematical sociology, your next task is to turn them back into words, so that people can interpret them. So in fact the semiotics of data collection, administration, manipulation and so on, are riddled with questions of representation. Each time we decide to count something, the 'thing' is also a word, and hence subject to contestation via its definition, salience, and use. And each time we arrive at an understanding based on quantitative methods, we have to explain them in natural language – back to definition, interpretation, and contestation.

NW: *Cultural studies has a bad press in Britain and possibly elsewhere in the world. Why do you think that is?*

TM: In Britain it's often regarded as a 'Mickey Mouse' subject – that's actually the language used. You find plenty of people invested in the elite universities such as Oxford and Cambridge decrying it. You get people within media institutions like the BBC or *The Guardian* decrying it. You get plenty of people who are worried about so-called 'standards of education' decrying it.

Cultural studies is going through the same growing pains and denunciations that sociology did after the Second World War, that literature did in the late 19th century, and that the natural sciences did in the early 20th century. In other words, when you have massive imperial and economic changes to the way in which a country functions, the knowledge which is generated in universities to deal with those transformations has trouble getting a place at the table amongst those who have been trained in other domains.

If you went back a century and a bit to look at the way that English literature was denounced as 'Mickey Mouse' – though unfortunately they didn't have Mickey in those days – by contrast with Ancient Greek and Latin, you'd find extraordinary similarities.

In the US, cultural studies is associated much more with literature. So the historic task of high culture, its Arnoldian/Reithian mission in British terms, was to elevate the citizenry. That is supposedly being thrown to the wolves by literature professors, who instead of understanding that vocation, are instead obsessed with dross. In the US, the criticism is that obsessions with political correctness and the popular are diminishing the capacity to undertake the historic mission of literature: offering a disinterested view of human interaction and the social world that is about mythic quintessences rather than conflicts, classes, or genders.

NW: *It doesn't follow that because something is despised now, it has value that will emerge as history unfolds.*

TM: You're absolutely right, and of course we're in an era when areas like academic publishing are changing very rapidly; the interrelationship of the media and universities is changing very rapidly; and the commodification of knowledge is changing very rapidly. And unless cultural studies manages, on the one hand, to satisfy some of those requirements and modify itself to the prevailing political economy, and on the other hand, to find methods, forms, and norms that are legible to more traditional university areas, as literature managed to do, it will have difficulties.

But if we go back to the 1950s, to C.P. Snow, the great physicist and novelist, and his 'Two Cultures' pamphlet, he lamented the fact that whether he was in Knightsbridge, London, or Cambridge, Massachusetts, when he spoke to literature professors, they didn't understand anything about laws of thermodynamics, whereas physics professors knew something about T.S. Eliot. Snow felt as though 'ne'er the twain shall meet'. One of the benefits that cultural studies might offer if it manages to get friendly with the sciences and the social sciences is that it is actually very interested in how those things can intersect.

Let me give you an example that's organic and already happening. In electronic games, people in cultural studies can write code and understand how software and hardware interact, and people in computer science are interested in narrative and understand the imagery of different subjects. These people take the same drugs, wear the same clothes, sleep with the same people, and go to the same parties – and are no longer either physically or symbolically at opposite ends of campus. So if cultural studies can follow that kind of example, without losing its commitment to the questions that I've adumbrated, to do with subjectivity and power, it may have a future.

NW: *Do you think the point of cultural studies is to understand things or to change them?*

TM: Ah, this is your inner Marxist expressing itself! Those things are deeply connected. If you look at what people do who teach public policy, or tourism, or shipbuilding, or architecture, or history, guess what — they are not just finding out truth for its own sake. They're actually deeply complicit with, and implicated in, the nature of the economy, how people are trained to participate in it, how state work is done, and the knowledge citizens have, that helps make them the people they are. So there is no pure, unscarred form of knowledge that doesn't try to change things.

FURTHER READING

Richard Maxwell and Toby Miller, *Greening the Media* (Oxford University Press, 2012)

Toby Miller, Nitin Govil, John McMurria, Richard Maxwell and Ting Wang, *Global Hollywood: No. 2* (University of California Press, 2011)

3

LAWRENCE SHERMAN ON CRIMINOLOGY

 Lawrence Sherman is Wolfson Professor and Director of the Institute of Criminology at the University of Cambridge, and Distinguished University Professor in the Department of Criminology and Criminal Justice at the University of Maryland. He is also Honorary President of the Society of Evidence-Based Policing, a 2,000-member group of police professionals and scholars committed to applying social science research to police practices (www.sebp.police.uk), and Chief Executive of the Cambridge Centre for Evidence-Based Policing (Cambridge-ebp.net). His books include *Policing Domestic Violence* (1992) and *Evidence-Based Crime Prevention* (2002).

Nigel Warburton: *There are many theories about crime, its causes and treatment. So how do we decide which policies are effective? Take the case of restorative justice, when criminals and their victims meet face to face. Some critics argue that this approach is too soft on perpetrators and doesn't work. But is this true? Lawrence Sherman of the University of Cambridge believes that theories about crime can and should be put to the test. He's a passionate advocate of experimental criminology.*

David Edmonds: *The topic today is experimental criminology. I guess we'd better start with a definition of criminology itself.*

Lawrence Sherman: Criminology is the science of law-making, law-breaking, and law-enforcing. My own work is to develop criminology as the primary science for making better decisions about how to make laws, how to respond to law-breaking or to prevent it in the first place.

DE: *You're a pioneer of experimental criminology. Tell us what experimental criminology is.*

LS: Experimental criminology is a field that is defined in part by its method, like experimental physics, or experimental biology. For most of its history, criminology has been essentially a descriptive or observational science, like astronomy. We don't think that we can intervene in the way the planets revolve around the sun – the big dispute used to be whether or not they did. In science there are always important descriptive questions. But in medicine, the descriptive questions translate very quickly into prescriptive questions. How do you treat sick patients? How do you prevent people from getting sick in the first place? By developing a field of experimental criminology we accept that the core concerns of criminology have to be how societies make decisions and what decisions they should make to deal with their crime problems. That goes well beyond the descriptive, the observational and the purely theoretical. It requires having very hard empirical evidence, especially randomised control trials, which is the primary method in experimental criminology.

Fifteen years ago I founded the Academy of Experimental Criminology. Now we have a *Journal of Experimental Criminology* and we have a division within the American Society of Criminology. We even have the 2,000-member Society of Evidence-Based Policing, designed to promote the conduct of experiments in policing and the use of the experimental results in structuring police practices and improving police methods. There's no reason why you couldn't have a society for evidence-based corrections or evidence-based prosecution. Prosecutors are about the most reluctant group to get involved in experimental research; they, more than any other part of the criminal justice system, tend to think that they have all the answers. Evidence-based sentencing is very big; there's a lot of interest from judges now who think that it's unethical for them to be sentencing people without knowing the likely consequences of their sentencing decisions.

This is all coming together to reframe criminology, and to expect criminology to provide the same kind of interventionist guidance that medicine provides, as distinct from biology or chemistry. Criminology is both an interventionist science and an observational science.

DE: *So are you dragging the rest of criminology with you on this mission? Or is most criminology still practised in the old descriptive style?*

LS: Most criminology is still observational, as well as critical. Most criminologists today will have been heavily influenced by the role of social science in the late 20th century as a source of social criticism and as a source of values that were contrary to conventional values at the time – greater tolerance for diverse lifestyles, greater human rights – lots of good things. A book like *The American Dilemma*, by Gunnar Myrdal, helped Americans get to grips with the fundamental immorality of the segregationist laws in the United States which were being challenged in the 1960s. That's when police research first became visible, and my PhD supervisor, Albert J. Reiss, Jr., carried out systematic observations of things like police arresting black people more than white people and there being more police brutality against black people. And that's really what drew me into the field. The fact that his research was documenting all this helped us to accept that there were problems and that we had to do something about them.

But in my own career development, I was very fortunate in having the guidance of an observationalist scientist to help me become an experimentalist. My teacher, Al Reiss, never did an experiment in his career, but he encouraged me and gave me good advice about how to do experiments, in part because I had the chance to do it. I had spent some time as a research analyst in the New York City Police Department before I earned my PhD. That cocktail of practical experience with social science at a high level has been the basis for me pursuing and promoting this agenda of interventionist criminology, which means experimental criminology.

DE: *Give me a couple of examples of experiments you've carried out.*

LS: By 1981, my former supervisor in the New York City Police Department had become the Chief of Police in Minneapolis.

At my request, he obtained unanimous approval from the Minneapolis City Council to randomly assign arrest. It was the first randomised clinical trial in the world, in the use of arrest. It was in the context of police not having made arrests for misdemeanour, domestic violence, common assault, and a new Minnesota law that gave them the power to make arrests even if they hadn't witnessed the offence. We got approval to enlist 40 police officers to act as doctors would in a randomised control trial, randomly assigning their patients to different treatments. Now there's some criticism in criminology of calling an arrest a 'treatment': it's a sanction, it's a step in the process leading to a potential prosecution. But from the standpoint of the individual who gets arrested, it can be an intervention that changes their life, for better or worse.

DE: *So in this trial, some people were arrested after allegations of domestic violence, and others were merely warned at the scene of the crime, and there was a randomised approach as to who got which treatment. Then you looked at the effect of that?*

LS: We did. There was actually a third option which was that the police would ask the offender to leave home for the night. The lowest repeat offending rate over the next six months was the group that had been arrested, and this made head-lines all over the world. It provoked changes in the law in 28 US states and became policy in the UK and Australia. Other places, too, were convinced by what was seen as good news: that a scientific experiment had shown the wisdom of a retrib-utivist policy that was both morally satisfying and empirically effective. The bad news was that you have to replicate a finding like this to be certain of its generalisability – and this one turned out *not* to replicate.

DE: *So it worked in one specific part of the United States, but didn't work elsewhere?*

LS: That's right. In the early 1980s, Minneapolis was a booming economy, with a low unemployment rate. When we went to Milwaukee, which has high structural unemployment and racial segregation – a large area of Milwaukee is inhabited by a black underclass with very low employment rates – we found that when you mix arrest for domestic violence with unemployment, either for individuals or in neighbourhoods of high unemployment, it backfires. In these circumstances, arrest doubles the risk of repeat offending. This contrasted with the effect in the neighbourhoods that had high employment, where arrest was an effective deterrent. So we begin to see a connection between the social context of individual offending and the effects of an intervention, just as there's some evidence in medicine that certain medicines work well for some people, or in some contexts, but very badly in others. And it's this sort of specification that experimental science is capable of, whereas theoretical science can't do it on its own – it's got to follow the experiments.

DE: *But is that not a problem for the entire discipline? Because, presumably, there are so many causal factors involved in crime that you'll never be sure that your experiment can be replicated in the next town, let alone the next country.*

LS: This is true in other kinds of science. Darwin famously took 20 years to publish – a lot of people, including some distinguished sociologists, thought that that was because he was uncertain, and they cite him as a great scientist who was purely observational. But they don't know Darwin's work. What he was doing for 20 years was experiments, and he needed, in his own view, to have those experiments confirm his proposed laws of natural selection.

DE: *In that first arrest experiment you found powerful effects within a six-month period. But how do you know that the results will survive longer than that? It's not practical, is it, to repeatedly return to the same people?*

LS: Well, the possibility of doing that is actually quite great, and while we didn't do it in Minneapolis, we have followed up the 1987/88 experiment in Milwaukee over a 23-year period. Milwaukee was the experiment in which we first found that the effect of arrest depended on whether the suspect was employed. The question was how long would that last? Many other things happened in their lives: they can get arrested for other crimes, there can be a change in economic conditions etc. Most theorists, I think, would assume that the impact of a randomly assigned arrest in 1987 or 1988 is unlikely to persist for 23 years. They would be wrong. In fact, the effects got bigger after around 12 and 15 years, and the negative effect of arrest on repeat domestic violence of unemployed people is the most powerful persisting crime effect. There's no positive benefit from arresting employed people that lasted 23 years. And quite apart from repeat offending, the victims were significantly more likely to die (of all causes) if their abusers had been arrested than if the abusers had been warned. In the long run, at least in Milwaukee, the strongest effect of arrest was to shorten the lives of victims, who died sooner of heart disease and other internal causes.

DE: *The arrest experiments are fascinating. Can you give another example of an experiment you've been working on?*

LS: Yes. In the mid-1990s, the Australian National University asked me to help design a test of a very old method of dealing with crime, now called restorative justice. This has been the traditional basis for justice in the Middle East, among the aboriginal Canadian tribes, and in many other parts of the world, in which the primary purpose of justice is not to do what Immanuel Kant described in the 18th century – namely, to inflict a just measure of pain, no more no less, than what each individual deserves for the seriousness of their transgression. The traditional purpose of justice, instead, was to repair the damage to relationships, that allowed marginally-existing communities to go on existing. There's a long-standing human, almost evolutionary, process of trying to work out how to resolve a conflict which has been created by a crime that disrupted a relationship.

That's the context. What was the experiment? Well, the police in Canberra identified people who they thought might be appropriate for a meeting among the victims, their families, the offender and the offender's family. Instead of prosecuting them in court, the offenders would be diverted to this meeting, led by a police officer. At the end of the meeting there would be an agreement that the offender would do something to try to repair the harm to the victim. But prior to getting to that point, there would be a very robust discussion in which the offenders would have to begin by saying in front of this group what they did. And these efforts succeeded not only in getting offenders to describe their breaking of the law and the harm that they caused, but also, in most cases, the offenders would voluntarily apologise. Then there would be a discussion about how they could either do community service or, in some cases, direct personal service. But the victims didn't really want the money or the compensation. They mostly wanted the apology.

DE: *You mention that the police experiment was successful. But how was success defined?*

LS: Well, in the short run, the success was holding a conference. This didn't happen in 100% of the cases, but it did happen most of the time. And then having everybody walk out of the conference saying, 'Yes, this was a good thing to do', that was a success. And according to the victims, they felt much better having gone to the conference and they certainly felt much less angry than victims who didn't have a chance to have this kind of conference and apology. The offenders felt terribly ashamed and there's some evidence that offenders were even traumatised by the conferences. The offenders were actually reliving the conference in the days, months, years ahead, having nightmares about how angry some of the people were in the room.

DE: *Is that a good outcome!?*

LS: Well, it's possibly part of the causal process for less crime – a means to an end, where the end appears to be less repeat offending. We have pretty good results across ten randomised control trials that are on a par with the best tests for rehabilitation programmes for offenders, which are carried out at much greater expense, after prosecution, and sometimes after prison. The best you can get by way of reducing repeat offending is something we achieved without ever taking these people to court; so much cheaper, much quicker and with far higher levels of victim satisfaction.

After four of these experiments in Australia, the British government invited us to test the same method, but at a different stage of the criminal justice process. From 2001 to 2005 we ran eight experiments in Britain, which were supplements to prosecution, not substitutes for it. The results were quite comparable. Overall we reduced repeat offending, measured by convictions, compared to the control group, by close to

30% within two years. I don't think there is a rehabilitation programme in the UK that works that well, and certainly not for the very low cost of engineering this kind of meeting.

The long-term follow-up will be informed by what we have learned about how offenders have reacted to this kind of conference. There has been a knee-jerk opposition by conventional criminal-justice policy-makers to the use of restorative justice as appearing too soft and as something the tabloid papers would criticise – and few politicians in a democracy would ever want to offend the tabloid newspapers. But it's not a soft option. It's an option that's much more potentially damaging, psychologically, than just sitting in your prison cell and having your lawyer do all the talking for you. It is damaging psychologically in the sense that it is painful in the moment, not necessarily damaging in the long run. We have had people who've led miserable lives, one of whom has written a book about his experience in restorative justice. This experience got him out of a career of 5,000 burglaries. As far as he's concerned, even though he still remembers the trauma of that conference, it's the best thing that ever happened to him.

DE: *What kind of skills do you need to be a really good experimental criminologist? You're required to come up with a hypothesis about what will work, so presumably you need to draw on various disciplines: economics, psychology, and so on?*

LS: Well, criminology itself is a multi-disciplinary field. It's one that has competition from economics, psychology, and sociology. These are all fields in which journal articles are published with crime as one of the measures of the study. But criminology is like a sponge. We welcome the basic science disciplines to do what they're interested in doing. Very often it's to prove a theoretical premise. The economists are fond of showing that punishment works because it fits a rational-choice model. Daniel Kahneman has blown that model completely out of the water in terms of how people really do make decisions. His notion is that you can 'nudge' people into different decisions, for example by working with inertia and changing whether they have to tick a box on a questionnaire to go one way or the other, or by making it more likely they'll pay a criminal fine by sending them a text message. This approach is called behavioural economics, but it also belongs in experimental criminology because it uses identical methods. These methods give us information about how to undertake interventions to get people to obey the law, to comply with legal punishments at the lowest cost to the tax-payer, to make a safer and more just society, but also to use as much soft power as possible, and not to use harder power than is really necessary. We wouldn't be thinking that way if it wasn't for behavioural economics and psychology and other fields that we then incorporate into experimental criminology.

DE: *You've been working with governments and police organisations around the world. Aren't you worried about getting your hands dirty, about taking money for research and somehow losing your objectivity?*

LS: Fortunately, as long as your salary comes from a university, I don't think you have to worry about losing objectivity. There's a lot of hand-wringing in criminology about chasing government grants and whether your objectivity is thereby compromised. But in criminology something interesting is going on right now. We've been doing experiments without central government grants, especially in the UK. When the local police department wants to do an experiment and they call up the university and ask for help, you don't charge them any money or not very much money, but they put in an amazing amount of resources, sometimes even including the data analysts who gather the data and work on the study. So it's a different model. It's a model that gets away from any party-political interference with a crime policy. Domestic violence is a good example: in the United Kingdom, the party-political view of it has been mandatory arrest is the only thing you can do. The central government haven't allowed the kind of experiments we've done in the US. Well, now you've got local control of police departments in the UK, and all sorts of experiments are possible, and if one police and crime commissioner doesn't want to do the experiment, you can go to another.

DE: *Crime remains stubbornly high despite these experiments. Is that a sign of the failure of experimental criminology?*

LS: The evidence is against your premise. Serious crime in the
United States and the United Kingdom has been falling substantially in recent years and the most common reason that
police chiefs give for that in the United States is that they've
been concentrating police patrols in hot spots of crime, at
hot times. I'm very pleased to say that our research was
something that appears to have launched all that.

First of all, in Minneapolis we discovered that 3% of the street
addresses produced over half of all the crime. So that was a
descriptive observational statement. Then there was a predictive statement: we said that the places that were hot last year
were going to be hot next year. Historically, police tried to give
all of the community, all of the landmass, equal attention. But
that's like treating patients who aren't sick. So we developed
this idea of hot-spots policing which would concentrate police
resources in a small number of places where most of the crime
was occurring and at the times when crime was occurring.

The first randomised control trial on this was in Minneapolis.
Chief Anthony Bouza persuaded the city council to allow
him to take police cars out of low crime neighbourhoods
and put them into the high crime hot spots, and on average,
over the course of the year, we doubled the level of patrol.
Police cars used to be in hot spots about 7% of the time: it
went up to 15%. The difference in the crime rate was about
two-thirds: there was a 50% reduction in robbery in the hot
spots, for example.

There have been over 20 experiments replicating this result
and they pretty consistently show that you push crime
down in the hot spots if you can double patrol time. There
is somewhat less consistency, but still an overall positive
result, suggesting you do not displace crime to the areas
nearby that hot spot. There is more complexity about the
question of whether you displace offenders to different
kinds of crimes or to locations far away. That question is
almost metaphysical, because if they go to New Zealand
from Minneapolis, we're not going to know it. But what we
can take heart from is the great accumulation of evidence
now, the replication of the medical model, of repeated
experiments producing pretty much the same good news.

That is now part of what we're doing in Trinidad, where the homicide rate is roughly 40 per 100,000. In the past there has been greater use of patrol in the daytime than in the evening, but most of the homicides occur between 6p.m and 2a.m. With a new commissioner there, there's been a strong push for evidence-based policing, drawing on experimental criminology, and we're in the midst of a randomised control trial to see if we can get a big reduction in violence and serious crime, using this preventive strategy.

I'm optimistic about the basic approach of altering environments and measuring very carefully whether the changes in the environments can reduce crime over a long time. That's what happened with public health with clean water and clean air and other environmental strategies that, in a sense, are trying to put doctors out of business. Well, they'll never be out of business completely; but fewer people getting sick, more people living longer, people living longer because they're not getting murdered – you can see there's a very close connection between criminology and public health.

DE: *And is that what motivates you? Is it the impact on policy and people's lives, or is it the intellectual puzzle, the working out what works and what doesn't?*

LS: All of the above. You can't undertake this work without having a profound curiosity about how it all fits together, and then for me, what you can do about it. Why would we want to understand more? Certainly because we're curious, but also because we want to make a difference. A lot of people who are curious about something are happy to stop when they can explain it. Other people like to come up with a strategy, but they don't want to test it. Winston Churchill once said that it's very important that any strategy, no matter how beautiful, can actually be examined to see if it's working. And I like to take the whole journey, from understanding and explanation, to predicting that a certain intervention will work, and then testing whether that prediction is correct, reformulating the theory if necessary, and then testing the intervention. Using all this we can build up a body of evidence that in the long run will help us to have the safest societies in human history.

FURTHER READING

Lawrence W. Sherman and Heather M. Harris, 'Increased death rates of domestic violence victims from arresting vs. warning suspects in the Milwaukee Domestic Violence Experiment', *Journal of Experimental Criminology* 11(1): 1–20 (Springer, 2015)

Lawrence W. Sherman, Heather Strang, Evan Mayo-Wilson, Daniel J. Woods and Barak Ariel, 'Are restorative justice conferences effective in reducing repeat offending? Findings from a Campbell systematic review', *Journal of Quantitative Criminology* 31(1): 1–24 (Springer, 2015).

Lawrence W. Sherman, *The Rise of Evidence-Based Policing: Targeting, Testing and Tracking* (Center for Evidence-Based Crime Policy, 2013) http://cebcp.org/wp-content/evidence-based-policing/Sherman-TripleT.pdf

4

JONATHAN HAIDT ON MORAL PSYCHOLOGY

Jonathan Haidt is a social psychologist and Professor of Ethical Leadership at New York University's Stern School of Business. He is author of *The Happiness Hypothesis* and *The Righteous Mind* and is currently writing a book about morality and capitalism.
Photo: Mathieu Anselin

David Edmonds: *Abortion, capital punishment, euthanasia, free speech, marriage, homosexuality: these are all topics on which liberals and conservatives take radically different views. But why do we adopt certain moral and political judgements? What factors influence us? Is it nature or nurture? Are we governed by emotion or reason? Jonathan Haidt, a psychologist and best-selling author, most recently of* The Righteous Mind, *was formerly a staunch liberal. His research has now convinced him that no one political persuasion has a monopoly on the truth.*

Nigel Warburton: *The topic we're going to focus on is moral psychology. Morality is normally studied in philosophy departments, not psychology departments. What is moral psychology?*

Jonathan Haidt: Philosophers are certainly licensed to help us think about what we *ought* to do, but what we *actually do* is the domain of psychologists. We study many different aspects of human nature including morality, moral judgement, moral behaviour, hypocrisy, and righteousness. These are major topics of huge importance to our political and everyday lives.

NW: *For a psychologist this, presumably, involves experiments, or at least observation?*

JH: That's right. It involves scientific methods which don't have to be experimental. As with any difficult-to-study field, it's appropriate to use a range of different methods including fieldwork, reading widely, talking to people who have varying moral world views, and so on. In that sense it can be a little bit like anthropology.

NW: *In recent years there have been some interesting developments now that MRI scans can give us a glimpse of what's going on physiologically when people are making decisions.*

JH: Yes. There are two aspects of this. First, to acknowledge that moral judgements arise from events in the brain. But the more interesting questions are about which parts of the brain are particularly active when we're making them. It turns out that, from Joshua Greene's original study, and Antonio Damasio's before that in the 1990s, that brain regions associated with emotion play a very large role, and the reasoning areas sometimes take a long time to come in. One of the big topics of debate now is how to fit those together: the fact that we reason logically, we feel emotions; the frontal insula is more active when we're disgusted. I'm on the side that says that emotional reactions tend to drive the reasoning, and I think most of the neuroscience literature is consistent with that.

NW: *Most of us like to think that when we make a moral decision, it's somehow a rational decision, it's not just a gut instinct. Are you saying that's a kind of self-deception?*

JH: Yes, I am. We judge right away. This is one of the major findings in social psychology; it's sometimes called 'the Automaticity Revolution'. It goes back to Wilhelm Wundt 120 years ago. Within the first quarter of a second we react to people's faces, we react to words, we react to propositions, and then reasoning is much slower. Robert Zajonc, a well-known social psychologist, argued in the 1980s that 'preferences need no inferences'. For example, our minds react to something new as if to aesthetic objects, and then that reaction constrains the nature of our reasoning. What we're bad at doing is sizing up all the evidence and seeing where it points overall.

What we're really good at is saying 'Here's the hypothesis I want to believe; let me now see if I can find evidence. If I can't find *any* evidence, alright, I might give it up...' But wouldn't you know it, we're usually able to find some evidence to support it.

NW: *So, you're saying that moral reasoning is really just rationalisation?*

JH: For the most part, when we are doing moral reasoning about anything that is vaguely relevant to us. Some people think that I deny that rationality exists, which I don't at all. We're able to reason about all sorts of things. If I want to get from point A to point B I'll figure it out, and then if somebody gives me a counterargument and shows me that, no, it's faster to go through C, I'll believe him or her. But moral judgements aren't just about what's going on in the world.

Our morality is constrained by so many factors: one of the main ones is our team-membership. Political disagreements have a notorious history of being impervious to reasons given by the other side. That then makes the other side think that we are not sincere, we're not rational; and both sides think that about each other. What you think about abortion, gay rights, whether single mothers are as good at parenting as married couples: all of these attitudes tie you to your team, and if you change your mind, you are now a traitor, you will not be invited to dinner parties, and you might be called some nasty names.

NW: *What's your evidence that moral judgements aren't rational?*

JH: I first got interested in this sort of question in graduate school. I was reading a lot of ethnography about how morality varies across cultures. In culture after culture they had moral rules – about the body, about menstruation, food taboos – and I was reading the Old Testament, and the Qur'an, and all these books, and so much of this morality seemed visceral, hard to justify in a cost–benefit analysis. It's true that utilitarians say 'Actually, they're just wrong; morality is really about human welfare, and all we have to do is maximise human welfare.' If most people were intuitive utilitarians, then I think you could say that; but what you find is that people are not naturally utilitarians. Again this is not to say utilitarianism is wrong. I'm just saying that people have a lot of moral intuitions, and experiments on persuasion show it's very hard to persuade people.

My own research involved giving people scenarios that were disgusting, or disrespectful, but caused no harm. For example, a family eats their pet dog after the dog was killed by a car in front of their house. When confronted with that scenario, the Ivy League undergraduates did generally say that it was OK – if they chose to do that, it was OK. So there was one group that was rational utilitarian in that sense, or rights-based I suppose you would also say. But the great majority of people, especially in Brazil and *especially* working class in both the US and Brazil, said 'No, it's wrong, it's disrespectful, there's more to morality than this.' So just descriptively, most people have moral intuitions that conflict with utilitarianism. When you interview them about these, or if you do experiments where you manipulate their intuitions, you can steer their reasoning to reveal the intuitions.

NW: *I know you've divided the kinds of intuitions they have into five categories. Would you mind just recapping those?*

JH: What really struck me when I was reading all this ethnography, and when I spent three months doing research in India, is the degree to which certain patterns are so recognisably similar all around the world, yet the final expression of a morality is so often unique and so variable between cultures.

What are the underlying patterns that can be explained from an evolutionary point of view? Reciprocity is a strong candidate here. Robert Trivers wrote a famous article on reciprocal altruism. If someone wants to claim that fairness and reciprocity are entirely socially constructed, entirely learned from our parents, that is just implausible. The same applies to caring for vulnerable offspring. We're mammals, and we have mammalian tendencies. So you start with those two aspects, reciprocity and caring for offspring, and recognise that nativism has to be right about those. The categories that my colleagues and I added are group loyalty – we're good at coalitions; respect for authority; and then the fifth one is sanctity or purity – the idea that the body is a temple. This is just descriptive, not normative. Those are the five that we feel most confident about, but there are many more. Nowadays we think liberty is different from the others. I think in the future we're going to find that property, or ownership, is a moral foundation; you see it all over the animal kingdom with territoriality, and there's some new research from several labs showing that children at the age of two, or three, notice and care about property and ownership and what's in someone's hand versus not in their hand.

NW: *One of the interesting insights in your research was the way that, politically, liberals and conservatives are attached to different sets of values.*

JH: That was not my original intent. I was investigating how culture varied across countries, especially the contrast between India and the United States. What I found in my early work was that social class was sometimes an even more important factor than nationality. That's what I set out to study, and that's how my colleagues and I arrived at this list of moral foundations. I was engaged in this research on morality when the Democrats lost in the 2000 US elections, and then lost again in 2004. I was a fairly strong liberal back then: I really disliked George W. Bush. I wanted to use my research to help the Democrats understand, to help them connect with American morality, because George Bush was connecting, and Al Gore was not. So when I was invited to give a talk to the Charlottesville Democrats in 2004, right after the election, I took my cross-cultural theory and applied it to Left and Right, as though they were different cultures. It worked well. I expected to get eaten alive: I was basically telling this room full of Democrats that the reason they'd lost was not because of Karl Rove, and sorcery and trickery, it was because Democrats, or liberals, have a narrower set of moral foundations – they focus on fairness and care, and they don't understand or communicate the group-based, visceral, patriotic, religious, hierarchical values that most Americans have.

NW: *That seems to imply that you helped Democrats to play to virtues or types of moral thinking that didn't come naturally to them. It's almost as if you were suggesting they should be insincere in the way that they put themselves across.*

JH: I began simply by wanting the Democrats to win. It was an open question whether the advice would be that they should assume a virtue whether or not they had it. But I changed what I felt as I went on. I treated this like ethnographical fieldwork. I would read conservative magazines; I subscribed to cable TV so I could watch Fox News; and at first it was offensive to me, but once I began to get it, to see how the views interconnected, how if you really care about personal responsibility, and if you're really offended by leeches and mooches and people who do foolish things, then you don't want others to bail them out. If those are your values, then I can begin to see how the welfare state is one of the most offensive things ever created. So, I started actually seeing what both sides are really right about: certain threats and problems. Once you are part of a moral team that binds you together, it blinds you to alternate realities; it blinds you to facts that don't fit your reality. So, I was writing Chapter 8 of *The Righteous Mind*, where I tried to explain conservative notions of fairness and liberty, and I handed it to my wife to edit. I told her that I couldn't call myself a liberal any more, because I really thought both sides were deeply right about different issues.

NW: *That's very interesting. So the connection between your empirical research and your own changing personal political beliefs was fairly direct.*

JH: That's right. If you're studying morality, you're studying the operating system of our social life. Since the operating system of academia is very liberal, or leftist, I was enmeshed in the liberal team. I was trying to help my team win as an activist would. We have a lot of debate in social psychology, whether it's acceptable to be an activist, because we have many social psychologists who are activists, especially on race and gender issues, and most people think that's alright. But I've come to think that it's not. Once you become part of a team, motivated reasoning and the confirmation bias are so powerful that you're going to find support for whatever you want to believe. I'd like to think that my research, eventually, helped me leave my team and become a free agent.

NW: *Do you want to generalise from your own experience? Or are you saying that social scientists ought to remain aloof from politics?*

JH: I'm saying that if you are a partisan, you are not going to process reality evenly. Good science doesn't require that we all be neutral and even-handed. The way science works, the reason why it works so brilliantly, is not because scientists are so rational; it's because the institution of science guarantees that whatever we say is going to be challenged. As long as we have a working intellectual marketplace, as long as there's somebody to take the other side, someone to try to refute what we're saying during the peer review process, then science can be full of biased individuals. The problem is if everybody shares the same bias, there's nobody on the other side, and it is likely that the group will reach conclusions that are simply false. That's what's happened, not on most issues, but on some politically charged issues of race, gender, and politics.

NW: *One thing that's noticeable in your work is the way you use metaphors. How important are metaphors for you?*

JH: I believe we are intuitive creatures that are not persuaded just by logic: things have to feel right first, and then we look for supporting evidence. If it feels right *and* we see the evidence, then we believe. I'm trying to persuade people and say 'Look, here's how the mind works, here's how morality works'. I therefore have to offer them not just a whole list of experiments – every science book does that – but I have to give them some metaphors to help them change their mental structures, and then have a place to put all these experiments that I then summarise. So, my first big review article, published in 2001 in the *Psychological Review*, was titled 'The Emotional Dog and Its Rational Tail'. I was trying to make the case, based mostly on a review of the literature, not my own research at that point, that intuitions drive reasoning, not the other way around. So that's a metaphor that I put out there in the title of my paper and that seemed to stick: a lot of people seemed to gravitate to that.

The second metaphor that I suggested that's had some currency was for my book *The Happiness Hypothesis*. I developed the metaphor that the mind is divided into parts, like a rider on an elephant, where the rider is the conscious, reasoning, verbal-based processes, 1 or 2% of what goes on in our heads, and the elephant is the other 99%, the intuitive automatic processes which are largely invisible to consciousness. That's the best metaphor I ever developed; I hear from people all the time: 'Oh yeah, I read your book; don't remember anything about it, but man, that metaphor, that stuck with me forever, and I use it in my psychotherapy practice.' And then in *The Righteous Mind* I've added a few more metaphors: one is the idea of hive psychology, the thought that we human beings are products of individual-level selection, just like chimpanzees, that make us mostly selfish; and we can be strategically altruistic, but that we also have this weird feature, which is that under the right circumstances, we love to transcend ourselves, our self-interest, and come together like bees in a hive. These are some of the best times in our lives; these are incredibly important politically, in terms of people joining causes and rallies. So, the metaphor that I developed in *The Righteous Mind* is that we are 90% chimp, and 10% bee.

NW: *You're a psychologist by training, and psychology is usually thought of as one of the social sciences. Is that how you see yourself, as a social scientist?*

JH: Yes. I study morality, I identify as a social psychologist. But because I focus on a topic from multiple perspectives, I find that some of the best things I've read have been by historians, economists, anthropologists, and philosophers, especially those philosophers who have been reading empirical literature. I think of myself as a social scientist, almost as much as I think of myself as a social psychologist.

NW: *Is there something distinctive about being a social scientist, as opposed to being a scientist, or a philosopher?*

JH: The natural sciences form the prototype of what we think the sciences are. If you're studying rocks or quarks, and there's this definitive experiment, and you design this experiment and get the results, it's very clear, it's easy to understand. But rocks and quarks do exactly what the laws of physics tell them to. The social sciences are necessary because our subjects have these properties of consciousness and intentionality. There are these emergent properties that rocks and quarks don't have. Studying people and social systems requires a different set of tools and different ways of thinking, and you can't avoid questions of meaning. For the natural sciences, meaning is not a relevant concept, but it is unavoidable in the social sciences.

FURTHER READING

Jonathan Haidt, *The Righteous Mind: Why Good People are Divided by Politics and Religion* (Allen Lane, 2012). Many readings and resources related to the book can be found at www.RighteousMind.com

Paul Bloom, *Just Babies: The Origins of Good and Evil* (Bodley Head, 2013)

Christopher Boehm, *Moral Origins* (Basic Books, 2012)

5

ROBERT J. SHiLLER ON BEHAViOURAL ECONOMiCS

Robert J. Shiller, the recipient of the 2013 Nobel Prize in economics, is a best-selling author, a regular contributor to the Economic View column of the *New York Times*, and a Professor of Economics at Yale University. His books include *Finance and the Good Society*, *Animal Spirits* (co-written with George A. Akerlof), *The Subprime Solution*, and *The New Financial Order*. He lives in New Haven, Connecticut.

David Edmonds: *You have a choice: buy this plastic alarm clock right next to where you are standing for $28 or walk ten blocks and buy it in another shop for half price, $14. Now try this one: buy a laptop for $1995 in the shop next to you or walk ten blocks and get it for $1981. The chances are you are more likely to walk to save money when buying the cheap clock than the expensive laptop, which is odd because in either case you could save exactly the same amount of money. In the past 20 years there has been a revolution in economics with the study not of how people would behave if they were perfectly rational, but of how they actually behave. At the vanguard of this movement is Robert J. Shiller of Yale University.*

Nigel Warburton: *The topic we are going to focus on is behavioural economics. Now, we know roughly what economics is, but what's behavioural economics?*

Robert J. Shiller: Well the word 'behavioural' refers to the introduction of other social sciences into economics: psychology, sociology, and political science. It's a revolution in economics that has taken place over the past 20 years or so. It's bringing economics into a broader appreciation of reality. Economics was more behavioural 50 or 100 years ago. At Yale University where I work, 1931 was the year when the Department of Economics, Sociology, and Government was split into three separate departments.

NW: *Why would it matter if they just split the departments up? There's an argument that specialisation allows people to progress further in their field and is preferable to knowing a little bit about everything.*

RS: Absolutely. There are both advantages and disadvantages of this structure. The advantage is that we develop mathematical economics and mathematical finance to a very advanced level – and that's useful: we have option pricing theory that is very subtle and allows complex calculations that have some relevance to understanding these markets. But it loses perspective on why we have these options anyway. It offers a justification typically that involves rational behaviour. You can get into the swim of that, thinking 'I want to know why smart people use options.' It's instructive to go through the exercise of thinking 'Is it really ever right to buy these investment products?' But that doesn't mean that you're answering the question why people *really* do buy options, and why this market exists, and why other markets that sound equally plausible don't exist.

NW: *So what you're saying is that traditional economics has focused on an ideally rational individual, asking 'What would such a person do if he or she behaved in their own best interests based on the information available?' But behavioural economics brings in the fact that we don't always behave in our own best interests.*

RS: That's right. Conventional economics misrepresents what our best interests are. A great example is the financial crisis that began in 2007. The way it began was home prices started falling rapidly. Many people had committed themselves to mortgages and now the debt was worth more than the house was worth; they couldn't come up with the money to pay off the mortgage, and it led to a world financial crisis. So why did that happen? Conventional economic theory can't seem to get at the answer, which I would say is that we had a speculative bubble driven by excessive optimism, driven by public inattention to risks of such an eventuality, and errors in managing the mortgage contracts that were made. There are no errors in conventional economics: it's all rational optimisation.

NW: *Well let's take the optimism that you described. Many people were incredibly optimistic about the never-ending increase in house prices. There's a sense that they were just ignoring past oscillations. Is that a basic trait in human beings, that we are particularly optimistic: when we see things getting better we think they are always going to get better? Or is it something very specific to this case?*

RS: It's always more specific to the case; it depends on framing how you think about the problem. Kahneman and Tversky, two psychologists very important in behavioural economics, talked about the so-called 'representativeness heuristic'. We tend to look for patterns in the data that we think are representative of history. And we have salient images of things that have happened, like home prices always going up: they've always gone up in our lifetime. You might look for some break because you also have another model in your mind, which is 1929, and the stock market crash. So you have people looking for these patterns. While home prices were going up and up it just seemed as if anyone who raised the observation that they might fall wasn't making an intuitively plausible observation. Until they started falling! The other template that's in their mind suddenly becomes real and then that causes a self-reinforcing drop. The amazing thing is that in the economics profession of 20 years or so ago there were no bubbles. Now people freely say 'bubbles' but it was one of those words that was considered unprofessional by economists because markets are smarter than any of us and anything that happens in the market has a rational explanation.

NW: *If we bring psychology back into economics in relation to the current crisis, what particular light would psychology shed on that? You mentioned people's optimism. Is it that there's a kind of herd mentality and the markets mirror that? Or is something else going on?*

RS: There's a lot going on. It turns out that the human mind is very complicated. Economic theory likes to reduce human behaviour to a canonical form: the structure has been, ever since Samuelson wrote this a half-century ago, that people want to maximise their consumption. All they want to do is consume goods; they don't care about anyone else. There's neither benevolence nor malevolence. All they care about is eating or getting goods and they want to smooth it; they described it in terms of so-called 'utility functions through their lifetime', and that's it. That is such an elegant, simple model, but it's too simple. If you look at what psychology shows, the mind is the product of human evolution and it has lots of different patterns of behaviour. The contributions that psychologists make to economics are manifold.

NW: *One that I know you've discussed is that a notion of fairness might trump economic rationality.*

RS: A sense of fairness is a fundamental human universal. It's been found in some recent studies that it even goes beyond humans, that higher primates do have some vestigial or limited understanding of fairness and equity. In terms of how the market responds to crises, economists assume that everything is done purely out of self-interest. And yet non-economists, when we ask them about how things work – they have a totally different view. In one of my questionnaire surveys we asked something like this: If the economy were to improve, what would your employer do?

   A) Nothing – why should he or she help me just because the economy goes up?

   B) Well, if the economy were to improve, that would mean the market for my services would improve, so my employer would realise out of self-interest that he or she would have to raise my wage in order to keep me.

   C) My employer is a nice person and he would recognise that he or she should share the benefits with employees.

   I gave this question to both economists and non-economists. The economists all picked B, or, rather, most of them picked B. They thought that market forces would dominate.

Whereas very few of the non-economists did: they thought either their employer was a bad guy which is A, or their employer was a nice guy, and that's C. So there's a different worldview, and I think that if people think that fairness is such an important thing in labour contracts then modelling the world as if it's of total insignificance is wrong.

B12. Please evaluate which of the following theories about the effects of general inflation on wages or salary relates to your own experience and your own job: [Circle one number]

1. The price increase will create extra profits for my employer who can now sell output for more; there will be no effect on my pay. My employer will see no reason to raise my pay.
2. Competition among employers will cause my pay to be bid up. I could get outside offers from other employers, and so, to keep me, my employer will have to raise my pay too.
3. A sense of fairness and proper behavior will cause my employer to raise my pay.
4. None of the above or no opinion.

	1	2	3	4	
US All	26%	11%	21%	43%	n = 112
Economists	4%	60%	11%	25%	n = 75

Source: Cowles Foundation for Research in Economics, Discussion Paper No. 1115, 1996

NW: *So doesn't this just make everything much, much more complicated because you can't reduce individuals then to some kind of cipher where they are simply maximising their self-interest in terms of economic benefits?*

RS: That's why a lot of economists don't like this. Maybe with some justification they'll say that there are too many details in this theory: you can't explain anything with it. But I'm unpersuaded by that criticism because, first of all, we can work on this and study people more, and understand what psychological principle is relevant. And, secondly, it doesn't help to have a theory based on wrong assumptions.

NW: *I can see this would work retrospectively because you've got much more of the data. But in terms of prediction it must be extremely difficult to know the features of psychology triggered by the particular situations that people find themselves in, and how people are then going to react, not just individually, but en masse.*

RS: This goes back to whether economics is an exact science or not. Alfred Marshall, the great British economist of the turn of the last century, said that 'Economics cannot be compared with the exact physical sciences: for it deals with the ever changing and subtle forces of human nature.' Think about predictions of the crisis that started in 2007: most economists didn't see it coming at all. It seems to me that the fault was that they didn't want to use their intuitive perceptions of how people are thinking; it seems to me that something crazy was going on: we were in a housing bubble. But that term was proscribed in professional discussions, as that's what the taxi driver says; that's not professional. Economists ask for proof. And I can't prove it. I can refer to survey data, but that's not solid enough. Economists just sometimes don't see the obvious; they don't rely on mental faculties of human judgement that they have, as well as not relying on a broader view of people that's informed by psychological or sociological research.

NW: *Is that because economists tend to see themselves as 'hard' scientists, as opposed to the 'wishy-washy' soft end of social science?*

RS: I think the economics profession suffers from physics-envy, I really do. We all wish we could be Einstein. It's too strong a model: we can't all develop the theory of relativity. The world of people isn't like that. When you look at what happens for example in a financial crisis, you've got to get immersed in a lot of detail. It doesn't become understandable by abstract economic reasoning. This means you have to look at an impression of what's driving people, what's on their minds, what they don't know, what the lawyers did with the contracts, what the people are assuming the government might do if such and such happens. It involves a lot of real world thinking which doesn't fit with the Einstein model.

NW: *What's so amazing about Einstein was that he made a bold hypothesis that was then to some extent corroborated later. Couldn't economists do that? Can't you have a mathematically generated hypothesis that's then either proved to be correct or not?*

RS: That's an interesting question and I've never been asked that
              before. I know Einstein wrote his special theory in 1905 and
              it wasn't until 1919 when they did an experiment involving a
              solar eclipse that Einstein was vindicated. So is there an
              example like that in economics? What springs to my mind is
              usually the opposite. Economists will see empirical regularities
              in the data and become famous for having named some empir-
              ical regularity and then shortly after that it stops happening.
              And so that's the reverse.

NW: *It's interesting that with Einstein the prediction couldn't possibly
              make the results happen. But in economics, conceivably, it could.*

RS: Yes. That's because economics deals with people. One of the
              great concepts in economics came from the sociologist Robert
              K. Merton who in the 1940s wrote an article called 'Self-
              fulfilling Prophecy' – he coined that term in the 40s. That's
              exactly what the Great Depression was: a time when people
              became pessimistic about the economy and they stopped
              spending, so that made it happen. It also refers to a reason
              why economists are loath to predict depressions, because
              they feel that it's anti-social to set in mind a course of thinking.
              Central bankers, especially, feel reluctant to do that.

NW: *I can see that somebody could predict a depression and it happens,
              but they might be wrong about the real causes. They can be accurate
              about the outcome but without having an adequate explanation
              of why it occurred, because of the complexity of a real situation.*

RS: That's right. First of all, important recessions come rarely, so
              in your career as a social scientist it might come once or
              twice. Secondly, there will be many people who will have
              predicted it, perhaps 20, but all for different reasons, and you
              can never figure out after the fact which one had the correct
              reason. There's a shortage of data. I'm talking about a particular
              problem in macroeconomics, especially when we have global
              recessions. Global recessions don't happen that often, and
              when they happen they are really big, and that's not something
              that any scientific method involving statistical analysis can handle.

NW: *So what, then, is the value of behavioural economics?*

RS: We are learning amazing things about human behaviour
              from behavioural economics, and also from neuroscience.
              The profession advances by bringing in insights from other

professions. The place where 20 years ago I would least have expected this is from the medical school. But people from the medical school are now coming into economic seminars because they go back to their laboratories and they perform an MRI or single-neuron study and see what's happening inside the brain. It used to be that we had no insight; we believed in what Samuelson called 'revealed preference'. We would look at how people's minds functioned by observing what they would choose to do in their economic life. But now we can look inside the brain and see something going on. The combination of behavioural economics with neuro-economics is going to be a very productive field in the next 20 years, and it's going to change our thinking about the economy.

NW: *Well, given all these different developments in the social sciences, in psychology, in neuroscience, does that make it more likely that economists are going to be good at predicting the next crash?*

RS: Economists' analyses should inform better public policy and so reduce the frequency of crashes. We don't want to have these crashes in the first place. And so they will be unsung heroes who saw something coming and averted it. It's just like the guy who designed the traffic lights and prevented numerous accidents. You don't go to this person thankfully saying 'You prevented my accident'; you don't even know that the person prevented it. So that's the kind of world I envisage, one where economists will fade into the background, just like the street planners in the city, and yet be doing good things.

FURTHER READING

George K. Akerlof and Robert J. Shiller, *Animal Spirits* (Princeton University Press, 2009)
Robert J. Shiller, *The Subprime Solution* (Princeton University Press, 2008)
Daniel Kahneman, *Thinking Fast and Thinking Slow* (Penguin, 2011)

SECTION 2

BIRTHS, DEATHS & HUMAN POPULATION

6

SARAH FRANKLiN ON THE SOCiOLOGY OF REPRODUCTiVE TECHNOLOGY

 Sarah Franklin is a Wellcome Trust Senior Investigator and holds the Chair of Sociology at the University of Cambridge, where she leads the Reproductive Sociology Research Group (ReproSoc). She is a Fellow of Christ's College.

David Edmonds: *In the sci-fi movie* Gattaca, *potential children are carefully chosen using pre-implantation genetic analysis. The movie taps into fears about the futuristic uses of reproductive technology. These are similar concerns to those often stoked in the press when there's a technological breakthrough such as the birth of the world's most famous sheep, Dolly, who demonstrated the possibility of cloning. Since the 1950s, sociologists have focused attention on such new medical technologies: IVF, cloning, stem cells and human embryo research are only some of the areas their research addresses. Sociologists in this field use a methodology very different from bioethicists; they stress what they call 'situated knowledges' or 'embedded ethics'.*

Nigel Warburton: *The topic we are going to focus on is the sociology of reproductive technology. Which kinds of reproductive technology most interest you?*

Sarah Franklin: Well I'm particularly interested in the modern reproductive technologies. I began my work on *in vitro* fertilization in the 1980s, and then I've gone on to study cloning, pre-implantation, genetic diagnosis, stem cell research – all of the reproductive technologies that involve reproductive cells, reproductive substance, and reproductive biology.

NW: *As a sociologist what is it that you do in relation to this? I can understand what a scientist of reproductive technology does, or a bioethicist, but I've not met a sociologist of reproductive technology before.*

SF: To a certain extent new methods have had to be developed for this field, which relies partly on qualitative methods such as participant observation and spending time in laboratories, conducting interviews with patients, with clinicians and scientists, and also investigating the public perception of these issues because that plays a large role in the sociology of this field. There are quite a few dominant narratives, or discourses, about what it means to consider the question of human cloning, or what it means to have a designer baby, so the methodologies that are used tend to combine work in the lab, interviews with people, with analysis of public debate, and examination of the issues in mainstream or popular culture.

NW: *It would be interesting to talk about that in relation to* in vitro *fertilization. I imagine you go into a laboratory and see people working with embryos or potential embryos, and sperm and cells and so on, but then what do you do? You observe them, presumably, and then what?*

SF: Well, IVF is a really interesting example because IVF really began in the 1960s. The first successful fertilization of a human egg was at Cambridge in 1969, and then it was quite a long time before it was clinically successful: it didn't succeed until 1978. After 1978 it began to be taken up and to become much more of a viable, clinical option. I don't think anybody thought in 1980 that there would be 5 million *in vitro* fertilization offspring by 2012. So studying this field has had to mean developing new methodologies as we go forward. My first study of *in vitro* fertilization simply asked women why they were undergoing that technique. In the mid-1980s when I began to research IVF, it failed 90% of the time. So the question of why that would be considered an attractive or a desirable option to be celebrated and pursued was itself of sociological interest.

I began by investigating that, and since then I've developed other ways of studying it. But my initial research was on what the technique meant for the people using it.

NW: *On that question I'd love to know what the motivation was for women undergoing that treatment in the early days.*

SF: I was really interested in the answer to that question too. I found something quite surprising because you would have thought that what the women I interviewed in the mid-1980s in Birmingham would say was that they wanted a baby, and obviously that was one of the motivations, but it wasn't the only motivation. They knew there was a 90% chance that if they used IVF they wouldn't end up having a 'take-home baby.' So what did they want? They wanted to know that they had tried everything so that in the future they wouldn't look back and think there was something else they could have done. But what they didn't anticipate, and what really no one can anticipate before they undergo IVF, is how demanding a procedure it is: how physically demanding, how emotionally demanding. So what they didn't anticipate was how the procedure would change them, how it would change their desire for offspring, how it would increase their proximity to the possibility of being pregnant. If they made it to the point where they had an embryo transfer, they had a fertilised egg inside their uterus, which, as far as many people are concerned, is very close to being pregnant.

Nevertheless, quite a few of the cycles that got to that stage failed. So, sadly, they often found that undergoing IVF took away from them exactly what they had hoped it would provide: instead of giving them reassurance it made it harder to live with the impossibility of becoming pregnant. That was one of the first aspects of IVF that really made clear to me how paradoxical it is; how it has a very self-evident logic for those going into it, but that exiting from it requires a much more complicated way of understanding what precisely IVF can offer.

NW: *Presumably what it can offer is changing over time as well, so the motivations will change and the impact of unsuccessful treatment will change.*

SF: Yes. I don't think anybody possibly could have imagined how quickly IVF would change. Initially, it was offered for various kinds of infertility: it was offered as a means of overcoming blocked tubes; it was offered as a means of repairing a process, of establishing a pregnancy. But IVF, both before it was used clinically and since, has become a platform for a much wider range of technologies. IVF was always a big technology in the livestock breeding industry, and embryo transfer is now a huge global industry used for improving the genetic capital of animals. But human *in vitro* fertilization quickly expanded into genetic diagnosis, into the diagnosis of male infertility. Now the major change with IVF is its close links with stem cell research. All the material for human embryonic stem cell research comes from IVF programmes, or very nearly all of it. So there's now quite a complicated connection between what we might call technologies of reproduction and technologies of regeneration. Oddly, too, IVF is now likely to be the platform technology for the future of regenerative medicine.

NW: *There's also the phenomenon that IVF is sensational news. There are caricatures of scientific practices that get transmitted through newspaper and television to the wider public. I wonder if that's something that you've investigated, the way that IVF is represented?*

SF: Certainly the mainstream representation of IVF is also one of the most fascinating things about it. Raymond Williams was very helpful in his analysis of television in giving us some ways to think about how public conversations take place about technology: he famously said that the impact of technology is one of the least understood and least well-theorised issues in all of social science. The reason he said that was because people already think they know what the impact of a new technology such as television is. It's notoriously difficult to theorise technology in relation to the question of impact, which after all is a term taken from physics. We wouldn't really expect any kind of simplistic model of technological causation to be sociologically credible, and yet that is what almost all models of technological change end up being. In mainstream debate they often tend to be future-orientated; they often tend to be relatively simplistic; they often tend to portray science and technology racing ahead without any control. Reproductive technology is a perfect example of that: it's a perfect example where the debates are often framed in terms of enhancement, designer babies, test tube babies and so on; but the reality of how decisions are made is much more complicated. One of the most important contributions sociology of this area can make is as an alternative to the dominant framings of technology, which don't take into account the social complexity of what is going on.

NW: *Well, let's take that notion of a designer baby, a kind of enhanced baby, better than you would have achieved by the traditional process of generating children. Is that really a myth? Is it really wrong to think that the technology is tending in that direction?*

SF: It's a really interesting question why reproductive technology became so closely linked to the enhancement question. I wrote a book about preimplantation and genetic diagnosis (PGD) with a colleague of mine, Celia Roberts at Lancaster University. We looked at a clinic in London where they were using the technology that involves both *in vitro* fertilization and testing the embryo for a known genetic disorder, and of course that technique is quite rare because in order to do a genetic diagnosis of an embryo you have to biopsy the embryo, and to do that you have to tear off a tiny cell and analyse the contents of that cell with a very high level of molecular precision within a very short period of time, because you have to decide whether you are going to allow that embryo to be used clinically, whether it's going to be transferred for an attempted pregnancy. If you are looking for just one gene it's very complicated and there's a significant error rate. So the idea that you could look for several is at present technologically unlikely, and even if you could, say, read the genes of the embryos, you'd probably get many conflicting pros and cons, as it were. The idea that you could then 'add in' genes and control how they are expressed is a way of *imagining* biological control that is actually racing ahead of the technology.

So rather than the technology racing ahead of the reality it is the other way around: these areas are beset with very high rates of failure; people who use them are really encouraged to think very carefully because they are difficult and time-consuming and very often fail. So the idea of the designer baby is a very powerful idea in public culture, but for people who are actually having PGD it's a very offensive idea because they are not trying to have designer offspring: they're trying to prevent a child suffering the consequences of a known and usually lethal genetic condition.

NW: *If somebody's known to have an inherited condition which could be prevented, that's very different when you intervene from somebody deliberately trying to engineer a particular kind of person in the Petri dish.*

SF: Yes, that's quite true. They're very different things. One of the unfortunate consequences of the huge emphasis on enhancement and on genetic engineering and the *Gattaca*-type scenario is that it makes it much harder for us to learn what is really going on. The future of all of these fields of bioscience, biomedicine, and biotechnology is going to involve difficult decisions. It's going to be very hard to know what's right and wrong in a certain situation. How should we decide, for example, what to do when it is possible to replace the islet cells in young people suffering from diabetes, but we know that it might actually be very dangerous and experimental for a long period of time to do so until that procedure works reliably? How do we decide whether it's right to subject children who have a survivable illness to some form of new medical therapy that could substantially increase their quality of life, but could also do the reverse? These sorts of questions are going to occur time and again in all different fields of medicine and science, and the people who are undergoing treatment now are arguably some of the most knowledgeable people about what those decisions involve: not just practically, or medically, or clinically, but ethically. One of the reasons why sociology is an important counteractive to the predominance of traditional bioethical ways of thinking about these questions (which often emphasise such issues as autonomy, and the right to know, or indeed the right not to know) is that although these are significant questions, they are not the only questions we need to ask. We need to decide how to make sense of a technology that gives a great deal of extremely precise knowledge and information but no clear indication whatsoever about how to use it, how to decide, who to consult, and so on. Sociologists and anthropologists in this area attempt to map the terrain and clarify the complexity. It would be a great contribution to widening the public debate on these issues if these kinds of studies could have a larger role.

NW: *Should that involve individual case studies as well as considering broader trends?*

SF: Yes. It should involve individual case studies, participating in public consultations and debates, and the kind of fieldwork I do where I'm sitting in the clinic where clinicians, scientists and patients, and whoever is around, come to talk to me partly because I'm not a clinical professional; I'm not a patient, I'm not a scientific professional. I'm there as a social scientist: I'm a person who's there making an effort of social description, working at a level of social analysis, working at an effort to think about these questions, and to make that thinking part of teaching, part of research and so forth. So that's really the work we are trying to do.

NW: *Would it be fair to summarise that as saying that you are trying to make sense of what's happening?*

SF: Yes, absolutely. Trying to make sense of it, and I often think of it as an exercise of collection. I'm trying to make sense of it by finding out how other people make sense of it. With that archive of different representations of the dilemmas that I've collected, I then try to represent back the knowledge that I've found. So my knowledge is really in conversation with other people's knowledge, and it's producing a different set of resources, really, to bring to the question of how to think about these questions and then how to resolve them.

NW: *If what you are doing is curating other people's experiences and describing situations, it's not obvious that will change social policy because it seems relatively neutral.*

SF: That's quite right. One way to describe the particularity of a sociological expertise would be that you are looking at the causes of the causes. So we have an idea of what the causes of, say, ethical uncertainty are, say, about a topic like cloning; but one thing the sociologist does that is quite different from what a clinician or policy-maker does, is they don't just go in and say 'Here's the problem; how are we going to solve the problem?' They say 'How did this definition of the problem come to be the definition of the problem that we are using to define this problem?' For example, the problem with cloning isn't necessarily 'Will humans be cloned?' In fact, it's entirely possible that humans may have been accidentally cloned already by various types of reproductive technology, and, technically speaking, the Dolly technique doesn't involve cloning because it involves a combination of different kinds of cells; whereas 'cloning' comes from the Greek word for twig. Cloning comes from viriculture because a fruit tree won't reproduce true unless you take a cutting. If you plant the seed of a grape it won't grow the same kind of grape: it's only if you take a cutting of a vine that you can get an exact genetic replica.

So cloning, a term from botany, means descent from the shared reproductive substance of one parent. That wasn't what the Dolly technique involved: the Dolly technique involved somatic cell nuclear transfer. It was a new means of trying to reproduce large numbers of cells that had a transgenic component. The idea was to introduce a human gene into sheep in order that the missing protein for people who suffer from a rare genetic disease could be extracted from the animal's milk. So really the questions we might want to ask about Dolly the sheep are quite old questions about reproduction and manufacture, and in a way how reproduction is becoming a form of manufacturing. Those are the kinds of questions that would be pertinent to the technique of making Dolly the sheep. The question of whether humans should be cloned, which was by far the dominant policy and media question that emerged from the announcement about Dolly the sheep, was, from a sociological point of view, from a historical point of view, not really the right question.

NW: *There's an interesting sociological question, then, about why those sorts of questions get a grip on the media, while other more accurate representations of what was going on don't.*

SF: I want to read the book on that. I really do want to read the book on how certain definitions of the problem become so widespread in the media, and the sociological explanation of that.

NW: *I was intrigued that you talked about 'manufacturing' as part of the technology of cloning. I didn't quite understand what you meant by that.*

SF: One of the really interesting things when you are in a laboratory where reproductive cells are being manipulated and handled, and literally being rebuilt, is that you are reminded of very traditional artisanal crafts. We associate something like the Dolly technique with a very high-tech, future-orientated science, which it is. But actually in the labs where those cells are being manipulated, people are, for example, making their own pipettes; they're making their own glass tools by hand over a tiny little forge; they will describe their tools elaborately. It's one of the best questions to ask in a lab: 'Why are you using that pipette?' because you'll get a very long explanation of precisely why the tip is the shape it is, and how they really prefer that to other ones, and what they are going to do with it. And all of this work is meticulous handiwork, really, that reminds us that although biotechnology is associated with new forms of commodification of the human, new bio-commodities and so forth, it's at a very early stage. It's really almost like agriculture before capitalism: it's like a very early form of capital, that's literally being handmade before it becomes scaled up. What we're seeing with IVF is the scaling-up stage; we're seeing it become franchised; we are seeing hedge funds invest in it; we're seeing a billion-dollar industry reach a whole new level of financial scale. Much of the stem cell sector is really prior to that. So I'm also very interested in the making of capital out of living cells: I'm interested in it as a technology, as an economy, and those are the kinds of questions that close attention to the laboratory can reveal.

NW: *What's the most important impact that the sociology of reproductive technology can have?*

SF: The importance of what are known as 'empirical ethics' is that they rely on methods that are used in social science that involve actual conversations with people who are embedded in a situation – participant observation interviews and so on – aiming to extract from those observations and from that data collection ways of approaching these questions that are based on what the people closest to them experience as the primary ethical issues. For example, it's a very significant ethical issue whether or not a clinic has a good freezing programme. If a clinic has a really good programme for freezing embryos it means that the couples who are undergoing IVF in the clinic have the option to freeze any excess embryos that they have that weren't transferred for clinical purposes, that weren't transferred to establish a pregnancy – because you can only transfer one at a time. If a clinic doesn't have a good freezing programme, the option for a couple to give those embryos to research would be in some ways more appealing because they wouldn't have the option of freezing them.

That's not an ethical question that you're going to see in a kind of mainstream discussion of what the key bioethical issues are for contemporary *in vitro* fertilization, because that's the kind of ethical issue that's really only going to make sense if you're personally in that situation. The lesson from this is that we really need to think more sociologically about what the ethical questions are, and where they come from. Similarly, we need to think more creatively about where the answers to the ethical questions come from, because they're not all going to come from philosophy; they're not all going to come from bioethics. Many of the answers to these questions – and indeed new kinds of questions altogether – are going to come from the people closest to these technologies, whose lives are most directly affected by them, and who have had quite complicated discussions about where the ethical issues come from, and what resources are relevant to addressing them. These include clinicians, scientists and patients, as well as sociologists who work in this area. The field in general – the field of sociology of reproductive technology – which is now a field that is about 25 years old, has helped to provide a different empirical base for thinking about the ethical challenges that are ahead of us, and that really is the most substantial contribution of the field. It will become increasingly apparent what a substantial contribution that has been.

FURTHER READING

Sarah Franklin, *Embodied Progress: A Cultural Account of Assisted Conception* (Routledge, 1997)

Sarah Franklin, *Dolly Mixtures: The Remaking of Genealogy* (Duke University Press, 2007)

Sarah Franklin, *Biological Relatives: IVF, Stem Cells and the Future of Kinship* (Duke University Press, 2013) – available as a free download here: http://oapen.org/search?identifier=469257;keyword=biological%20relatives

Sarah Franklin and Margaret Lock (eds), *Remaking Life and Death: Toward An Anthropology of the Biosciences* (SAR Press, 2003)

Sarah Franklin and Celia Roberts, *Born and Made: An Ethnography of Preimplantation Genetic Diagnosis* (Princeton University Press, 2006)

7

ANN OAKLEY ON WOMEN'S EXPERIENCE OF CHILDBIRTH

Ann Oakley is Professor of Sociology and Social Policy and Founding Director of the Social Science Research Unit and the EPPI-Centre at the UCL Institute of Education, London. She has worked in university social science research for more than 50 years. Her many publications span the fields of gender studies, women, health and reproduction; social science methodology; evidence-based policy; and biography and autobiography. She has also published seven novels. Her most recent non-fiction book is *Father and Daughter: Gender, Patriarchy and Social Science* (2014).

Photo: Theo Chalmers

David Edmonds: *Ann Oakley carried out pioneering work on women's experience of childbirth in the 1970s. Much of the data was collected through interviews. We interviewed Professor Oakley about her research and about the nature of interviewing.*

Nigel Warburton: *The topic we're focusing on is women's experience of childbirth. You did some research in the 1970s on this topic; could you say a little bit about that?*

Ann Oakley: Yes, I did, in around 1975–6. I was funded by what was then called the Social Science Research Council. It was a study of women's experiences of having their first babies, and I interviewed the women four times, twice in pregnancy and twice afterwards; with some of the women I was actually present at the birth as well. The focus of the study was the social and medical aspects of childbirth. It was partly about how the treatment of doctors affected the women after childbirth.

NW: *What sort of questions did you ask them?*

AO: Well, four interviews, two hours each, an awful lot of questions! The first interviews included many questions about the experiences of antenatal care. This was at a time when the treatment of women in childbirth was becoming a big policy issue in the media, and there was a lot of stuff in the newspapers about rising induction rates, etc. But there was not very much in the social science field about how the treatment of women in childbirth was actually experienced by the women themselves, and I wanted to fill that gap. So the first interviews were a lot about what it was like going to the antenatal clinic and what their expectations were about childbirth. Then, afterwards, I asked for an account of labour and birth, from beginning to end, and of course lots of questions about baby care, the domestic environment, about employment and the issue of going back to work, and about what was called 'postnatal depression'. I wanted women to talk to me about how they interpreted this term, whether they thought they had this thing called 'postnatal depression' and, if so, where had it come from?

NW: *How long after childbirth were you interviewing them?*

AO: This fourth interview was about five months afterwards, so, the researcher did quite a lot of holding the baby!

NW: *And were their husbands or fathers of the children present?*

AO: Sometimes, and sometimes they were there at the delivery, and sometimes I was there as well, and that was quite interesting. I won't say any more about that though...

NW: *So you had this huge archive of interview content. What happened to it?*

AO: I wrote a report for the Social Science Research Council, and I wrote two books. The first one was called *Becoming a Mother*, but the paperback version had a new title, *From Here to Maternity*. And the other book was called *Women Confined* and the subtitle was *Towards a Sociology of Childbirth*, and that was much more analytical. It was looking at models of postnatal depression and the interview data, and seeing how the existing explanatory models fitted with the women's accounts — which they didn't very well.

NW: *What was the existing understanding of postnatal depression that your evidence undermined?*

AO: There were two explanations in the medical literature at the time. One of them was that something had gone wrong with the women's bodies as machines — something had gone wrong hormonally. That explanation is still around. The other one was deficient femininity, and that came from the psychoanalytic domain. But what I found most interesting was that the accounts of the women I spoke to were not accounts of depression. They were accounts of exhaustion, sleep deprivation, the shock of being precipitated into a new occupation (a mother, often without any training); they were about exposure to surgery, to hospital institutionalisation, and all these things that we know are stressful for human beings. So you didn't need to have any special explanations of women as women, you just needed to understand that childbirth is a human life event and it can have these kinds of consequences.

NW: *I can imagine that's true for many women, but surely there must be some women for whom physiological/hormonal changes do trigger events of depression?*

AO: Yes. I think there were two or three women in these 55 who fell into that category. Around a third said that they had been labelled as having postnatal depression, and then, when probed about what this 'postnatal depression' felt like, gave accounts of 'I haven't slept for four nights'. In those days, women were kept in hospital for nine to ten days. There were all kinds of things which made that an uncomfortable time: having a routine imposed on you, listening to everyone else's crying babies, having the baby taken away and test-weighed if you were breastfeeding...

NW: *So did your research feed into policy at that point?*

AO: I'm not sure it fed into policy at *that* point, but it has been subsequently said that this research, and other research happening around that time, did draw attention to the fact that we need to listen to the recipients of maternity care.

We need to understand what it's like from the mother's point of view. This was the beginning of a period in which maternity-care policy became more sensitive to issues of choice and so on.

NW: *What inspired you to research this topic in the first place? Was it your own experience of motherhood?*

AO: I always say that in the vast majority of cases, the choice of research topic amongst social scientists reflects a mixture of the personal and the professional. And, yes, I was interested because I had had two children and had my third child during the project. But the intellectual origin of the project was in my previous research, which had been looking at women's experiences of housework. In asking questions about how gender worked in the home, it became clear that the point at which women's lives really changed was not marriage/ partnership, but the birth of the first child. After that, it became much more difficult to manage an equal partnership, and I think that is still true today.

NW: *Now, I know that you've returned to the childbirth research you did in the 1970s and reinterviewed some of the women you interviewed in the first study. Could you say how you tracked these people down and what the motivation was?*

AO: Well, first of all I did most of the first study as a sole researcher. But the follow-up study has been with a team of other researchers at the Social Science Research Unit. Of the original 55 women who were interviewed in the 1970s, we have found 36 to interview. Finding them has involved quite a lot of detective work, going through, first of all, the NHS tracing system, but also using other means. One of the irritating things about women is their habit of changing their names!

NW: *Did that raise any ethical problems? I know that with some social science research you have to go through approval committees in order to begin the tracking-down of individuals.*

AO: Yes, we did all of that. It took several months to get it through the relevant ethics committees. These didn't exist in 1975. That original project didn't go through an ethics committee. I simply wrote to a consultant at a local hospital and said 'I want to do this study' and went to see him. He said 'Yes', and then

I had access to the medical records. That would not happen today, quite rightly. I think it was outrageous really. I know I behaved ethically, but not everybody would. So one of the problems this time round was the ethics committee said 'Where are the original consent forms?' and I said 'We didn't have consent forms in 1975' – and there was a long silence while they took this information on board and worked out what to do about it. Some of the ways that it was possible to relocate the women involved finding their adult children on Facebook and grappling with the question 'Is it ethical to contact somebody through that kind of route?'

NW: *So, once you tracked them down, were they amazed that you wanted to speak to them again?*

AO: They were amazed. Most of them, I think, were really pleased. They've been very welcoming, meeting me at stations, inviting me to stay, providing meals, talking about everything. It's been a very heart-warming experience. Some people, when recontacted, really did not want to be taken back to that time, and said so. In one or two cases we were able to change their minds, ethically of course, but people have the right to say 'No'.

NW: *And what are you examining? Is it their recollections of those first few months of childbirth, or is it what happened subsequently?*

AO: It's both. The main emphasis is on how these experiences get remembered. Actually it has drawn my attention to the fact that there is very little work on the sociology of individual memory. It's very interesting how people remember things, and how each time you remember something you change it, and how sometimes what you remember is not what happened, but what somebody told you happened. So, moving on from that, we're interested in how they remember the first childbirth, and then we go on to whether they've had other children and how the subsequent experiences compare with the first one. Many of them are grandmothers, so we ask how they think things have changed for women generally, and then questions about all the other things that have happened over the long period since the first interviews. Many of these women are retired now, so they've got to go through 30 years of employment history and relationship changes, and all sorts of things have come up that we didn't really expect.

NW: *You've got a transcript of the original interview and I imagine, as regards the issue of memory, that it must be difficult to resist the temptation to correct people and say 'Well, no, no, that's not how it was'?*

AO: We didn't read the transcripts before we went, but, of course, I had done the interviews that we were re-doing, and I couldn't cut out my own memory. For example, I remember going to see one woman, and we had lunch after the interview in her house, and her husband was there, and he said 'Nice to meet you again' and she said to me 'Where did you two meet before?' Well, we met in the delivery room and she had forgotten that I was there.

NW: *This whole process is based on face-to-face interviews and almost participant observation, if you're in the delivery room. It's an unusual interview situation where something potentially traumatic, and certainly life-changing, has just happened or is happening to somebody. Did these interviews require special considerations?*

AO: Yes. The original interviews need to be located in the context of the time, and what people then said, wrote and thought about social science interviewing. Back then, when I look at the social science textbooks on methodology and the ethics of interviewing, I found they were extremely unhelpful, precisely because they did not cover those kinds of situations, in which there were longitudinal, face-to-face interviews about a very intimate, potentially traumatic subject. For example, one of the things that one textbook said was that the interviewer is a sort of mechanical data gatherer, and he (it was usually a 'he' in the textbooks) doesn't give away any information about himself. And the example that I quote in *From Here to Maternity* that drove this point home concerned a woman that I interviewed, who, at the end of the second interview, just before the baby was due to be born, said to me 'Now could I ask you a question?' And I said 'Yes', and she said 'Can you tell me which hole the baby comes out of?' Now, if I had been going by the social science textbooks, I would have said 'Mm, well you should ask your doctor that', but how could I not answer the question? That is an extreme example, but I got lots of questions. If you expect somebody to talk about themselves and their experiences, don't you have an obligation, an ethical obligation, to be prepared for that to be an interaction, rather than 'I'm the questioner, and you're the answerer'? It doesn't work like that; it's not the way things happen.

NW: *Given that you were moving away from conventional social science interviewing techniques by revealing things about yourself and interacting in a certain way with the people you were interviewing, did you feel tempted to disguise that fact when you came to write up your report?*

AO: Well, I don't think the report for the Social Science Research Council paid a lot of attention to this aspect of the interviews. I think the 1970s were the beginning of my realisation that researchers have an obligation to write up the research as they did it, and not give a sanitised account. But lots of researchers didn't do that, and consequently what they wrote were accounts that were essentially unbelievable. In *From Here to Maternity* there's a chapter on 'being researched', which has got some of the women's questions and raises some of the issues about this kind of interviewing. And then a colleague of mine, Helen Roberts, was writing a book on feminist research and asked me to write a chapter about interviewing women. Out of all my publications that chapter is the most quoted, and it caused quite a degree of controversy amongst feminist social scientists. It's complicated, but there's a class issue: I was a white, middle-class woman, so how did my biography impact on the data that I was getting? It started a debate, which is very good. The point of these things is not to close but to open a debate.

NW: *So looking back at what you were doing in the 1970s, if you began that research today, would you go about it differently?*

AO: I don't think so, but perhaps I'd be more sensitive to the boundary between a professional research relationship and a friendship. Purely from the research point of view I remember sometimes thinking, when I came away from an interview 'I really enjoyed that and I learnt to mistrust that feeling. If I enjoyed the interview, I wasn't attending properly to the questions, and I was anticipating replies too much, rather than extracting them or waiting for them. Well, there was no guidance; I really felt as though I was on my own.

NW: *Now, some social scientists see their work as in the same spectrum as the 'harder' sciences, as they're sometimes called. They are collecting data in an objective way. But it seems to me that in a lot of what you've done, the fact that it was you doing it will have affected the data that you collected.*

AO: I think that's true whoever the scientist is and whatever the data. If people, including laboratory scientists, were honest about how they collect data and where their personal experiences come in, we would recognise much more of a link. In fact there's a whole literature, mainly by feminist scientists, about 'hard' science, and how it's not quite as hard as people pretend. Every research project bears the imprint of the person who did it; there's no way you can get away from that. But I think you can try to be aware, and to document the ways in which it seemed that there was that kind of interaction.

NW: *Your interviews were based around asking the same questions of each person, so, to some degree what you collected could be compared and given some kind of numerical quantification. Is that how you treated the data?*

AO: It's one of the ways in which I treated the data. On the issue of postnatal depression we asked standardised questions about the women's mental health after childbirth, and you can get a score out of that, and indeed we did statistical significance tests, and so on, and looked at the association between factors. At the same time we looked in detail at their accounts. I don't buy this distinction between qualitative and quantitative. I think all quantitative work is qualitative and vice versa. I think it's an unhelpful distinction, and very much so in the social science research field.

NW: *Given that what you did in the 1970s was focused on a relatively small group of people in one place, do you think there's anything generalisable from that?*

AO: Well, I don't think it is generalisable to women giving birth in developing countries then and now. One can ask the same questions in different places, and to some extent that has happened. There has been a lot more research, mainly in Europe and in North America, asking these sorts of questions and coming up with not dissimilar conclusions. It's an open question in any research project how far one can generalise, and it's very important to be clear about the limits of generalisability. But, as I said before, it's about opening the debate.

NW: *And is that what you see as the great value of the social sciences, to open up a debate, or is it to provide evidence to change the world?*

AO: Both, of course. I am in this business, not to change the world – that's too ambitious – but to produce evidence that is relevant to policy-making and to practice. The ultimate aim is to actually improve people's lives. For me, the point of it all is not to theorise in an armchair kind of way: it's about having some kind of practical impact. And sometimes you have that by opening a debate, by making people argue, and by highlighting an issue, like the treatment of women in childbirth, that was not regarded as an issue before.

FURTHER READING

Ann Oakley, *Women Confined: Towards a Sociology of Childbirth* (Martin Robertson, 1980)

Ann Oakley, *Becoming a Mother* (Martin Robertson, 1979, reprinted by Penguin under the title *From Here to Maternity* in 1981 and 1986)

8

SARAH HARPER ON THE POPULATION CHALLENGE FOR THE 21ST CENTURY

Sarah Harper is Professor of Gerontology at the University of Oxford, Director of the Oxford Institute of Population Ageing, and Senior-Research Fellow at Nuffield College. Sarah has a background in anthropology and population studies and her early research focused on migration and the social implications of demographic change. Her current research on demographic change addresses the global and regional impact of falling fertility and increasing longevity, with a particular interest in Asia and Africa. Sarah serves on the UK's Council for Science and Technology, which advises the Prime Minister on the scientific evidence for strategic policies and frameworks, and chairs the UK Government Foresight Review on Ageing Populations. She edited the *International Handbook on Ageing and Public Policy* and is Editor of the *Journal of Population Ageing*.

David Edmonds: *People are living longer. Over the past generation, there's been a dramatic increase in longevity, and that will have dramatic implications, for example, for the cost of providing health services, and for how long we will all have to remain in work.*

Nigel Warburton: *The topic we're going to focus on is the population challenge for the 21st century. Now, what is that challenge?*

Sarah Harper: Well, I think what is interesting about population is that at the end of the 20th century we saw tremendous changes which are going to follow through over the 21st century. And basically our population is changing in size; it's growing very rapidly. We currently have about seven billion people on the planet. That has probably *doubled* in the lifetime of most adults in this country. It is going to increase – we think – to round about ten billion, and then it'll probably flatten out. It's changing in its density; we're all becoming far more urban. Currently, we have about half the world's population living in an urban area. That will increase to 75% by the middle of the century and to about 80–90% by the end of the century, where nearly everyone on the planet will be living in an urban area. Distribution of population is changing. We're becoming mobile in a different way; traditional migration patterns are changing; who migrates is changing; where they migrate.

And probably, I think, one of the greatest challenges is a massive change in the age structure of the population in so much, as across the world women are having fewer children, and as a consequence, as we're also living longer; the age composition of our population is changing. So, for example, by the middle of the century, for the very first time, there will be as many old people as there are young people on this planet.

NW: *That's a lot of information. And I'm really interested in how you know it.*

SH: Well, we have some very, very good demography databases. The United Nations, for example, nowadays has a pretty good collection of population statistics. But they vary. In some countries, the database from which the UN can draw its statistics is obviously not as good as in other countries. But I think what we can probably say is that we are now sophisticated enough in our analysis that we can pretty well get the *trends* right, but we often underestimate the pace. So, if I say that there are three main contributors to population: there are two big drivers. One is falling fertility (that's falling childbearing) and one is falling mortality (or falling death rates). We can pretty well project those forward but, as in the past, we quite often get the timing wrong. The third one is migration, and that's extremely difficult, and that's because obviously, year by year, month by month, day by day, people are making decisions and those decisions change; and, as a consequence, where they live and where they move to – it's much, much more difficult to estimate that. But if we put migration aside for a moment, although we have a lot of theoretical perspectives on where, and how, and why people move, we can say that in terms of falling fertility (the decisions women across the world make to reduce their childbearing) and in terms of falling mortality (that's death both across the life-course, and extending our longevity because we're living longer and longer) we can pretty well say, from the data we have at the moment, that these trends will probably continue.

NW: *So, globally, there are going to be more old people around, the further you go into this century?*

SH: Absolutely. But we have to be careful how we define 'old people', because currently, at the moment, we tend to take a very old view which is that 60/65 is when people go into old age. And a lot of that is based on historical decisions to have 65 as the state pension age in Europe. When 65 was chosen as the state pension age by Bismarck in the middle of the 19th century, half the European population was dead by 45. If you got to 65, you really were old. Now, half the European population has a really good chance of making it to 85. And if we look at the health status of European populations in particular – but also, obviously, North America and Australia, most OECD populations, Japan, Korea, for example – we can say that we are pushing back the onset of the disabilities associated with old age. So much so that by one statistic, the health profile of a 70-year-old man today is very similar to his father's when his father was in his late 50s.

So, in one generation, we really have pushed back the onset of disability. Definitely when I was a child, if people made it into their 70s, you thought 'great!' Three score years and ten was what we used to talk about. And both my grandparents on my father's side died in their 70s and everyone said 'great!' Now, in the UK and in many other OECD countries, if someone dies in their 70s, you feel that somehow they have lost a lot of their life. And that means we've had to redefine old age. And I think really old age probably now starts, for many people, sometime in their 70s. Or even, some people are arguing now, that we are able to work until we're 70 and therefore old age probably is our late 70s or early 80s. So, by that definition, you can say that actually the percentage of old people won't necessarily get any more. But if we keep it by the statistics that old age starts at 65 and youth finishes at 15 – that's the current UN definition – yes we're having more older people and far, far fewer children.

NW: *I'm still not clear whether the key factor that presents a challenge is that older people are less likely to be working, or that older people are more likely, as they get older, to make more significant demands on health services.*

SH: That is absolutely crucial. And both are correct. Let's go back a little bit because I think one of the myths we have is that the reason why our population is ageing is because we're living longer. That is true, but the *real* reason why – across the globe, with the exception of Africa, particularly sub-Saharan Africa (and we can maybe talk about that a little later) – women are choosing to have fewer children; childbearing is going down. And, as a consequence, the average age of the population is increasing because there are fewer young people in the population. And one way to think about this is that in some societies, for example Afghanistan and Pakistan, you have well over 40% of your population under 15.

Now, if we project those statistics to the end of the century and remember these are countries where you still have a very high (what we call) 'total fertility rate' – to put it very generally, the average number of children born to women of childbearing age – the projection is that this will come down significantly; that even in these countries, we will drop from round about 40–45% of the population being children down to probably below 15%.

So, one way of looking at it is that the old population pyramid is changing. In the old days, we had this idea of a real pyramid. This was fuelled by lots and lots of births at the bottom. And these were young people who would come into our societies and drive our economies. Now, as you have fewer children and in particular if you live longer, then you go eventually into a skyscraper. And if you model the current population of advanced economies, we've actually – more or less – reached the skyscraper. But in some countries where fertility has fallen very dramatically – like Japan or Korea – they're almost in a vase shape. So the first thing we say is that ageing societies have fewer people coming in to their societies to drive their economies, so much so that the OECD, for example, has recently shown that in OECD countries – within round about 2017 or so – there will be more people leaving the labour market than coming into it. When you put that together with the other side and say if we're going to still have people retiring in their 50s or 60s and then living long, long lives, we have the challenge for societies. We may have reduced the child-dependence but we're dramatically increasing the older dependence.

We've got to look at that section of life in two ways. Firstly, why are healthy, active people in their 50s and 60s leaving the labour market when their health profile would suggest that not all but the majority can still stay active and contributory probably until they're 70? But inevitably, even if we live longer and longer and medical technology and science comes in, most people are going to experience a period of frailty and disability at the end of their lives. So, the second question is: how long will that be? And if we enter a situation where, even if people are working until they're 70 and don't become frail until they're 85, if you then have 20 years of frailty – which is unusual today but more likely in the future – that is where the burden of dependency comes.

NW: *You've presented this ageing population as a challenge. But it could be an asset if it goes the right way, because presumably people accumulate experience, skills, knowledge, capacities to pass that on and contribute not just directly within the economy but also indirectly through childcare; through education; through supporting people going into careers.*

SH: I think that's exactly right. And interestingly enough, in the last 25 years, this debate has moved around from the *problem* of an ageing society to the *challenge* of an ageing society. And now people talk about the *opportunity*. If you like, the trend in demography is fixed. It's not surprising; we've seen it coming for quite a long time. I think it's happened faster in some parts of the world than we thought. But here, at least in advanced economies, we've had a lot of time to plan for this. And a lot of it is just changing behaviour, and policy, and political will to grasp what – as you say – is a tremendous opportunity. Europe had 150 years to go from being young to old; we became mature by the measure that there are more people over 60 than under 15 in our society at the millennium. In Asia, there'll be more older people than younger people by about 2040. And this is happening in about 25 years. So we had 150 years, but some parts of Asia and Latin America are going to do this in 25 years. So they have a much bigger challenge than us. But if you look at advanced economies, it is actually very possible, particularly if we are pushing back the onset of disability, to compensate for the lack of younger people coming in – and really to make it an advantage because, as you say, older people tend to have certain expertise, skills, and experience.

Now one of the problems, of course, is that demography doesn't change in a vacuum. One of my colleagues says, very wisely, that if we look at demographic projections and we think they're the only things that are going to change, and we forget of course that the whole of society will change over that time span – that's when we make the mistake. So the very time that we've had the ageing of the population in Europe, and to a certain extent in the States, we've had the growth of the youth culture. And one of the really big shifts that happened was at the end of the 20th century. So, another demographic driver: we had the baby boom generation coming through – that's the post-war rise that we found in the US and Canada, and, to a certain extent, here in Europe. And they were entering the labour market. What are we going to do with all these people needing jobs? Booming economies? Fine! Let's just cast out 'older people'! And the older people got younger and younger until we were encouraging people at 50 to take early retirement.

Now, that solved a short-term blip. However, we now say: a) we can't afford 40 or 50 years of retirement, either as individuals or as a society, and b) what about all those skills that we got rid of? So I think many employers now realise this. I think many governments now realise this. But, of course, we changed attitudes 20/30/40 years ago and now we've got to change them back. So many people say to me 'Ah, but I was looking forward to retiring at 50/55' and 'It's not fair that my generation's going to have to work' and I say 'Yes, but your parents were probably the only people who were able to retire in their 50s! Your grandparents didn't!'

I stuck my head above the parapet about five years ago at a conference and I said in my lifetime I think we will see state pensions start at age 70. Well, very shortly after that, David Cameron announced that the UK was going to start shifting state pension age up to 68. And in June 2014 the Australian government came out with a proposal, which was eventually rejected, that state pension age should be 70 – affecting those born after 1966. That's a huge leap. And they're not just doing it for pensions. I think they're doing it because of skills and experience and the need to retain these workers.

NW: *Presumably, politicians are doing this as well, because they're getting access to social science data – research that indicates the direction in which things are going.*

SH: I think that's very true. The social sciences, particularly in terms of social surveys, took a long time to take off. And in different countries, there were different forms of data. So, for example, here in the UK we've already had very good birth-cohort data, starting right back in 1946. We surveyed mothers and young children and followed them through. So our knowledge on children and how children have developed over the last 50 years here in the UK is very good. In the US, they have had mid- and older adult life surveys for far longer than we have. And so, they have a real understanding of later life. But now we are becoming sufficiently sophisticated that we have a lot of national survey material; we have the ability and the social science tools to be able to put this together. We do a lot of cross-referencing; we combine variables. And so, we're able to take the same kind of data from different countries with different welfare systems, different economies, different politics, and look at the trends that are happening in the population and the way that different policy agendas affect that. So, I would say, definitely in the last 10/15 years, our ability to really engage with good high-quality social science data across at least the developed world has increased tremendously.

NW: *Presumably, that's because of the combination of digital processing and the internet?*

SH: Yes, to a certain extent, the internet is a major factor. But without any doubt, digital processing has just transformed things. But also, I think, things have improved from a funding point of view. In order to do a serious longitudinal survey, you need real commitment from a funder. Say, you're going to do a survey every five years and you want four waves; you know you need 15/20 years' worth of funding. I think it took a while for the funding community to wake up and understand that in the social sciences, that was the kind of magnitude of funding that was needed.

NW: *Is it fair to say that in your work you are as much a scientist as you are a social scientist?*

SH: Definitely. I think social scientists *are* scientists. Particularly coming out of population studies or demography. Without any doubt, it is a very rigorous, mathematical subject that underpins what we do. I think even if we go into more qualitative research, really good, high-quality qualitative research can add tremendously to our understanding of some of the projections and findings from social survey research. I think it can be valuable in two ways. I mean, the traditional way is that you might do a large social survey and then you would use qualitative work to look at a case study which might illustrate your findings. The way I like to think of it is actually that the qualitative research is an ideal vehicle for *hypothesis-generating* – that you have some ideas; you try it out in a qualitative way; you gain depth of understanding. And then you can test it in a larger quantitative survey to find out how generalisable your qualitative material is. So, I see qualitative research contributing both to statistical social surveys but also to theory-, and concept-, and hypothesis-generating.

NW: *Ageing studies is, to me, a new subject, in itself. You've been projecting ageing population figures into the future. How do you see the subject itself projecting into the future? Do you think it will become a much more important subject than it's ever been before?*

SH: One of the things we try to do here at Oxford is really shift the debate. So, I worked on population studies; that was what I was interested in. First of all, I was very interested in migration, so my doctorate was on migration. Then I had a postdoc where I looked at the impact of the one-child policy on the changing age composition of China. And this was in the 1980s, so it was when the Chinese government already then was beginning to realise – at the end of the 1980s – exactly what it was potentially going to do to its population. One of the things about ageing research here in the UK was that it was very much dominated by social work and social administration. So, a lot of our research was concerned with ideas around health and social care. That was very, very important but it did tend to narrow the focus.

My own personal journey was that I went to work at the University of Chicago in the new Chicago Center on the Demography and Economics of Aging, which started in September 1994, which was the month I arrived. And that was because a brilliant man called Richard Suzman had this vision that he should set up a series of centres which would explore economics and demography in light of the ageing of the American population. He had already been instrumental in setting up what we call the Health and Retirement Survey. This was a big survey which, for the very first time, looked at the over-50s. People really hadn't been interested in the over-50s. We had nothing like it here in Britain. So, having worked there, when I came back to Oxford I wanted Britain to have the same kind of advantage and wanted to shift the debate away from policy, and health and social care – which we were very good at, and has a place – to look at economics and demography.

So, over the last 15 to 20 years, that is what we here at Oxford have tried to promote. We now have colleagues in Africa, Latin America, throughout Europe, Asia, where we try and shift the debate into the changing age composition of the world. In addition, myself and Tony Atkinson encouraged a longitudinal study to start here. That was the ELSA study – which is the English Longitudinal Study of Ageing. Out of ELSA, SHARE was born – which is the European study. And now, we have these ageing studies all over the world. So, I think population ageing really is a subject of the future.

One of the really big projects that we're working on here at Oxford, at the Institute, is on the high fertility-rates in Africa, and the fact that, although total fertility rates – that's child-bearing per woman – are coming down across the globe, in sub-Saharan Africa they're still high. Two-thirds of the world's countries are now near, at, or below replacement level: that's round about 2.1. Sub-Saharan Africa is on average between four and seven children. And that does have implications for the world's population – how large it's going to be, for resources, for empowering women, for the chances of some of these countries to move themselves out of poverty and away from high levels of infant mortality. Now that is as much about population ageing as it is about development, because if the African population starts to reduce its childbearing then, inevitably, its population will age. And the idea of this demographic transition, where we go from a young population – which we've had historically for centuries and centuries – to an older population, is really what I think the focus of this subject is all about.

FURTHER READING

Sarah Harper, *21st Century Population Challenges* (Oxford University Press, 2015)

Sarah Harper, *Ageing Societies* (Routledge, 2006)

Massimo Livi-Bacci, *A Concise History of World Population* (Wiley-Blackwell, 2012)

Thomas R. Cole, *A Journey of Life: A Cultural History of Aging in America* (Cambridge University Press, 1992)

9

STEVEN PINKER ON
VIOLENCE AND HUMAN NATURE

Steven Pinker is Johnstone Family Professor of Psychology at Harvard University. He has won many prizes for his research on language and visual cognition, his teaching, and his books, including *The Language Instinct*, *How the Mind Works*, *The Blank Slate*, and *The Better Angels of Our Nature: Why Violence Has Declined*. His most recent book is *The Sense of Style: The Thinking Person's Guide to Writing in the 21st Century*.
Photo: Rose Lincoln/Harvard University

David Edmonds: *The world is a violent place, and if you watch the television you presumably believe it's getting more violent. But it isn't: it's becoming more peaceful – at least according to Steven Pinker, distinguished Harvard psychologist and author of* The Better Angels Of Our Nature. *It's a phenomenon which he believes social science can explain.*

Nigel Warburton: *The topic we're going to focus on is violence and human nature. A lot of people assume that there is something fundamental in human nature that makes us violent. Is that what you believe?*

Steven Pinker: Yes, but that's only the beginning of the story because there's also something in human nature that can inhibit violence. So, although we do have violent inclinations, it doesn't mean we'll always be violent, because it all depends on whether they're successfully inhibited or not by our peaceable inclinations.

NW: *And the story that you tell in your book is that we've moved from a position of giving in to our inclinations, to, as a species, being far less violent than ever before.*

SP: That's right. Any time you quantify violence and plot the rates over time, you see an overall decline from the vantage point of the present. That raises the question 'Why were we so violent in the past?' and it raises the equally interesting question 'How did we get less violent in the present?'

NW: *Just before we go into the explanation, is it really true that we are less violent, because that seems counterintuitive?*

SP: It seems counterintuitive because people get their impression about how violent we are from the news. The news is systematically biased toward things that happen, as opposed to things that don't happen, and we know from cognitive psychology that people's sense of risk is driven far more by their memory of vivid anecdotes than by any set of statistics. When you think about it, if someone dies peacefully in their sleep at the age of 87, there's not going to be a reporter at the foot of the bed announcing it to the world; and if there's some major city that has not been torn by war for the last 35 years, you never see a camera crew saying 'Here I am in the capital of Angola, and for yet another year there's no war here.' When something does blow up, that does make the news. Since rates of violence haven't gone down to zero, there's always enough to fill the news, and so our subjective impressions are out of whack with the statistical reality.

NW: *But isn't there more going on there than that? Because we've seen two world wars in the last century; we have the technologies for killing which are dramatically more effective than anything ever previously invented. Surely, in the age of the nuclear weapon, there can't have been a reduction in violence.*

SP: There can and there has been. In fact some people causally connect them: the reason there's been a reduction in war is because the fear of escalation to a nuclear war, which would be unimaginably destructive, has scared leaders straight, so they don't even contemplate a war, given that it might escalate into a nuclear holocaust. I personally don't think that was the primary cause. We have the memory of the two world wars (and our memory is more acute for more recent events; I call this historical myopia: the closer to the present, the finer distinctions that you make), but we tend to forget all of the holocausts and conflagrations of earlier centuries, which could be remarkably destructive. The worst civil war in history took place in the 19th century: the Taiping Rebellion in China. The European wars of religion were proportionately as destructive, probably more destructive, than World War 1. The Mongol invasions, the fall of the Roman Empire, the collapse of various Chinese dynasties: each one of these could kill a proportion of the population that was in the ballpark of the world wars of the 20th century. Also, we tend to forget that the 20th century is 100 years, so we think of the two world wars, ignoring the fact that, to the astonishment of military historians, since 1945 big, rich, developed countries have stopped waging war on each other. We just take it for granted that France and Germany aren't going to come to blows, but that's a historically unprecedented phenomenon.

NW: *So in your book* The Better Angels Of Our Nature, *you've gathered the evidence of the decline in violence. So what's the cause?*

SP: There are a number of causes. One of them is the spread of the reach of government: if you outsource your revenge and justice to a disinterested third party, there will be less bloodshed than if you are judge, jury and executioner of the crimes against you. Each side thinking that it's in the right and the other side is the aggressor can lead to endless cycles of violence and blood feuds and vendettas, which a court system and police force can circumvent. There's trade and commerce: when there are opportunities to buy and sell (a form of reciprocal altruism), then other people become more valuable to you alive than dead, so over the course of history, since there's been a richer infrastructure of commerce, trade becomes more tempting than plunder. Another factor is the growth of cosmopolitanism: people travelling, or reading about other peoples at other times and places, looking into their lives, empathising with them, getting evidence that they are not demons or sub-human, makes it harder to make someone a mortal foe or vermin that has to be stamped out. And finally there's the overall growth of rationality, literacy, the accumulation of knowledge, reason, science – all of which can encourage us to treat violence as a problem to be solved. And just as we try to cure diseases or alleviate famines, we can figure out techniques of making violence less attractive. And, intermittently, that's exactly what we've succeeded in doing.

NW: *So, this kind of government, this increase in trade, cosmopolitanism, and also the increasing rationality, apparently, they're correlated with the decline in violence, but the correlation doesn't necessarily imply a causal story there.*

SP: That's right. There have been statistical studies that try to turn the correlation into a causal story by, for example, measuring a putative cause at Time 1, and looking at the incidence of war at Time 2, so at least you've got the cause preceding the effect. These are regression analyses, which hold constant, various nuisance third factors. There are also experimental studies where an independent variable is manipulated in a laboratory to test, at least on a small scale, whether particular measures reduce the likelihood of violence.

NW: *That's really interesting because you're moving from an analysis of history, to an empirical, testable situation, where you're controlling variables like a scientist traditionally has done. But human beings aren't that easy to treat in that way when we're discussing what has happened a long time in the past. So there must be some degree of probability here, rather than certainty, about the causal stories.*

SP: Absolutely, I think most philosophers of science would say that all scientific generalisations are probabilistic rather than logically certain, more so for the social sciences because the systems you are studying are more complex than, say, molecules, and because there are fewer opportunities to intervene experimentally and to control every variable. But the existence of the social sciences, including psychology, to the extent that they have discovered anything, shows that despite the uncontrollability of human behaviour, you can make some progress: you can do your best to control the nuisance variables that are not literally in your control; you can have analogues in a laboratory that simulate what you're interested in and impose an experimental manipulation. You can be clever about squeezing the last drop of causal information out of a correlational data set, and you can use converging evidence, the qualitative narratives of traditional history in combination with quantitative data sets and regression analyses that try to find patterns in them. But I also go to traditional historical narratives, partly as a sanity check. If you're just manipulating numbers, you never know whether you've wandered into some preposterous conclusion by taking numbers too seriously that couldn't possibly reflect reality. Also, it's the narrative history that provides hypotheses that can then be tested. Very often a historian comes up with some plausible causal story, and that gives the social scientists something to do in squeezing a story out of the numbers.

NW: *I wonder if you've got an example of just that, where you've combined the history and the social science?*

SP: One example is the hypothesis that the Humanitarian Revolution during the Enlightenment, that is, the abolition of slavery, torture, cruel punishments, religious persecution, and so on, was a product of an expansion of empathy, which in turn was fuelled by literacy and the consumption of novels and journalistic accounts. People read what life was like in other times and places, and then applied their sense of empathy more broadly, which gave them second thoughts about whether it's a good idea to disembowel someone as a form of criminal punishment. So that's a historical hypothesis. Lynn Hunt, a historian at Berkeley proposed it, and there are some psychological studies that show that, indeed, if people read a first-person account by someone unlike them, they will become more sympathetic to that individual, and also to the category of people that that individual represents. So now we have a bit of experimental psychology supporting the historical qualitative narrative. And in addition, one can go to economic historians and see that, indeed, there was first a massive increase in the economic efficiency of manufacturing a book, then there was a massive increase in the number of books published, and finally there was a massive increase in the rate of literacy. So you've got a story that has at least three vertices: the historian's hypothesis; the economic historians identifying exogenous variables that changed prior to the phenomenon we're trying to explain, so the putative cause occurs before the putative effect; and then you have the experimental manipulation in a laboratory, showing that the intervening link is indeed plausible.

NW: *And so you conclude that the decentring that occurs through novel-reading and first-person accounts probably did have a causal impact on the willingness of people to be violent to their peers?*

SP: That's right. And of course, one has to rule out alternative hypotheses. One of them could be the growth of affluence: perhaps it's simply a question of how pleasant your life is. If you live a longer and healthier and more enjoyable life, maybe you place a higher value on life in general, and by extension, the lives of others. That would be an alternative hypothesis to the idea that there was an expansion of empathy fuelled by greater literacy. But that can be ruled out by data from economic historians that show there was little increase in affluence during the time of the Humanitarian Revolution. The increase in affluence really came later, in the 19th century, with the advent of the Industrial Revolution.

NW: *Your book is very unusual in being so eclectic in its sources. Do you see yourself as a social scientist primarily, or are you a scientist, are you a historian? How would you categorise yourself?*

SP: By academic credentials, I am an experimental psychologist, which makes me, by inheritance, a social scientist, because many people subsume psychology under the social sciences. We psychologists, when given the choice, like to describe ourselves as scientists. Many universities have gone through a battle as to which dean should be responsible for psychology, and usually we lobby to be included with the scientists. I've been at several universities and my department has been in many different schools. In fact, at one university my department was in three different schools at different times: while I was at MIT, the psychology department started out in humanities and social sciences, moved over to their equivalent of a medical school, and then moved again into the science school. So there's no clear answer to the question of what a psychologist is. I'm certainly not a historian by training and I couldn't possibly pretend to be one, particularly when it comes to analysing primary historical documents and other source material. On the other hand, as a social scientist, I'm perfectly comfortable when it comes to numbers, regressions, and graphs, and so I concentrated on the historical accounts that had some degree of quantification.

NW: *And do you see that as being at the core of the social sciences, this concern with what can be quantified, what can be measured scientifically, rather than purely interpretatively?*

SP: The way I would put it is that the scientist's concern is with testing whether hypotheses are true or false. Quantification is a means to the end of determining whether your ideas are right or wrong, but it doesn't necessarily have to be numbers. It could be phenomena that are qualitative, on/off, 1/0, black/white. Much work in linguistics consists of qualitative distinctions that differentiate rival theories, so quantification is not a fetish.

NW: *It seems to me that we're living in a golden age for social science: suddenly there are all these books filling the bookshelves which are primarily social science and written by often very skilful writers. Is there something happening here?*

SP: There *is* something happening here, because social science used to be the most boring part of academia. One wag described social science as 'slow journalism', and wasn't it W.H. Auden who said 'Thou shalt not commit a social science'? It had the reputation of being banal, of just redescribing common-sense phenomena, and it lost prestige funding to sexier fields of knowledge like neuroscience. But that is changing: you see bestsellers based on social science, you see policy-makers, certainly in Washington, that came from the social sciences. One of the reasons is that whereas social science used to be bio-phobic – it set itself in opposition to evolution and neuroscience and genetics – now a new generation of social scientists just doesn't see a strict boundary between biology on one side and social phenomena on another. And the advent of 'big data' has made social science sexy to those with an analytic, quantitative mind. Because of advances in computing technology, particularly in storage, you can have terabytes of data hold interesting lessons if only you could analyse them – something that just wasn't true when we had computers whose disc sizes were measured in Ks instead of in Ts. I think also the social sciences are no longer atheoretical, no longer just describing statistical patterns. Because of the unification with the sciences, there are more genuinely explanatory theories, and there's a sense of progress, with more non-obvious things being discovered that have profound implications.

NW: *And yet, there is this sense that the social sciences are always biased in one particular way, so the author confirms their political persuasion by the sort of research that he or she does.*

SP: Well, that would be a sin, to the extent that that's true, and that's what the rules of the game are designed to minimise. If you are riding some political hobbyhorse, you still have to prove your assertions by testing them against data that everyone would agree is a valid test of your hypothesis, and if your pet political theory comes out bloody and bruised then that's just too bad. At least that's the way that the game should work.

FURTHER READING

Steven Pinker, *The Better Angels of Our Nature: Why Violence Has Declined* (Viking, 2011)

James L. Payne, *A History of Force: Exploring the Worldwide Movement Against Habits of Coercion, Bloodshed, and Mayhem* (Lytton Publishing Co, 2004)

Manuel Eisner, 'From swords to words: Does macro-level change in self-control predict long-term variation in levels of homicide?', *Crime and Justice*, 43(1) (University of Chicago Press, 2014)

SECTION 3

SOCIAL SCIENCE THROUGH DIFFERENT LENSES

LENSES

10

GREGORY CLARK ON NAMES

Gregory Clark is Professor of Economics at the University of California, Davis. His research interests lie in long-run economic growth, and in particular the degree to which demographic processes in the pre-industrial world continue to influence social life in modern societies.

Nigel Warburton: *What's in a name? Well, according to Gregory Clark, quite a lot. Surnames predict social position with remarkable accuracy. Social mobility follows universal patterns, and surprisingly only usually occurs very gradually over a number of generations. Why this should be so is an intriguing question, as is the question of whether it's something we should worry about.*

David Edmonds: *Today we're talking about names. That's an odd topic. How did you get into that?*

Gregory Clark: It was a complete accident. If you'd have asked me six years ago whether I would ever write anything about social mobility or about names, I'd have said 'no'. However, my earlier book, *A Farewell to Alms*, argued the rich out-reproduced the poor in pre-industrial England. Nicholas Wade, a writer for the *New York Times*, asked whether surname frequencies over time could prove this. That question made me ponder that surnames are an amazing link to the past that everyone carries. A link in some cases in England back to 30 generations in the past.

DE: *So you had a light-bulb moment when you realised that there was this huge mine of data to access?*

GC: It turned out to be a series of light bulbs. First, I realised that if names carry information about social status, the rate at which that information is lost from the social system is a measure of the entropy of the system and of the rate of social mobility – and that that measure could be applied across different societies. The second realisation was that the intense interest people have about their ancestors meant that, in the last few years, giant databases have become available, revealing the distribution of surnames, and the distribution of surnames amongst elites, in many societies, over many centuries. The third light bulb was to realise that all you needed to measure the rate of social mobility was information over time on the general distribution of surnames and the distribution amongst some elite.

DE: *And you've studied different countries and different time periods?*

GC: Yes. I started with England where I discovered surprisingly slow rates of social mobility. But then everyone has the impression that England is hidebound and locked in the past. So I researched all the way back to medieval England. The startling discovery was that there's been *no* change in social mobility rates between medieval and modern England.

            Then the move was to Sweden, where we expect to find a society with very high rates of social mobility. It has enormous government interventions designed to ensure social mobility. The startling information from Sweden was that the rates of social mobility are no higher than in modern England. What's more, in 18th-century Sweden the rates are as high as they are in modern Sweden.

            So that started me on a hypothesis, which is: social mobility rates are a social constant. Maybe there's a physics of social mobility. And that led to an investigation of a whole series of other countries.

DE: *That was your hypothesis. Did your findings vindicate it?*

GC: So far, yes. And the most extreme case was Communist China where in 1949 you had a revolution which sought to overturn the social order, which executed large numbers of the previous ruling class, and where many members of that class fled to Taiwan, Hong Kong, or the United States. Using surnames, what you observe is that maybe there's been a slight increase in social mobility rates, but the leadership of the Communist Party today disproportionately represents the elites under the Qing emperors!

DE: *This is an astonishing finding because, as you say, many people assume that the UK is very class bound. And compared to social-democratic Sweden or Communist China, you might expect it to have much lower rates of social mobility. But that's not what you've discovered.*

GC: No. The very strong surprise here is the constancy of the rate of social mobility. One nice example from Britain is Oxford and Cambridge. We can look at names that show up disproportionally in these universities in 1800 and see how quickly they have become more average. 19th century Oxford and Cambridge were gentlemen's clubs. You had to have Latin to get in, you had to attend particular elite schools, Church of England service etc. Today, Oxford and Cambridge have transformed themselves. They now use publicly available exams which you can take in every school in the country. They rely much less on interviews; they rely more on standardised measures. Astonishingly, they have not – by one iota – increased the rate of social mobility. Elite names that were there last generation are still much more likely to be there this generation. And one reflection of this is that if you have a rare English surname, and someone with that surname was at Oxford or Cambridge around 1800, you are now four times more likely than the average person to attend Oxford or Cambridge – that's predictable on the basis of that one piece of information.

DE: *For how many generations does this effect last?*

GC: One of the things that I should emphasise is that there is a universal tendency for status to regress to the mean. That's a comforting feature of society; no elite in any of our studies remains an elite forever, and no underclass remains an underclass forever. How long getting to the average takes depends how far away from the average you are when you start. In the case of England, we can observe some groups that are so elite that it takes 25 generations for them to become average. At the bottom end, it turns out it's harder to distinguish the real underclass groups in societies. But, even then, sometimes you're talking ten generations for a group to go from below-average to average. There's one exception to this rule: we can find some societies where elites don't obey this law. But that's associated with marital endogamy within the group. So, for example, the Copts in Egypt have been an elite since the Muslim invasions 1500 years ago and haven't shown much sign of regressing to the mean. And in India there's almost complete persistence of some elite groups. Again, this is associated with strong marital endogamy. So I should qualify my claim: in any society where marriage is not completely endogamous amongst elite groups, there will be regression to the mean.

DE: *Can I ask you about the methodology of this? Presumably, some countries have better data sets than others. And there must be problems comparing different generations. How do you go about resolving those sorts of issues?*

GC: Yes. In each country we had to grapple with problems of data interpretation. What we need for this method to work reliably is an unerring rule that you inherit the surname of your father. There have been many deviations. Swedes, for example, have very little loyalty to their surnames and there are many Swedes who change their name. Mostly, that's low-status surnames changing to higher-status surnames. But fortunately, in Sweden, the authorities maintain a register of every name and you can't change your name without legal permission from the tax authority. That allows us to do name-control and make sure that we are using names that are actually inherited. In a society like Britain, one of the traditional freedoms of the British is the ability to change their name any day they want as often as they want. But, interestingly, in Britain people have much more name fidelity. There are many unfortunate British names now – Sidebottom, Longbottom, Nutter – which people still hold onto, and they're not even associated with low status. Then there's Glasscock, Mycock, Hercock, Hiscock; people hold on to these names! And, for our purpose, that's a big advantage. But even so, there is some selected name-changing and we have to deal with that. Another problem is to gain access to information on name distribution. Some societies, like Japan, have a suspicion of public information; that makes it very hard. We need to know what the general name distribution is, and what it is amongst elites. England, increasingly, is moving to a society where it may become impossible to do this type of research. Because now, even to acknowledge that someone attended Oxford and had a particular name is not permitted under British information laws.

DE: *You concluded that social mobility does occur, but only over many generations. Both rich and poor eventually move towards the average, or mean. What are the mechanisms by which this happens?*

GC: For me, as a social scientist, this is the most interesting part of the story. The question that comes up is: is this a cultural phenomenon? Is it a familial culture that is being passed on? Is it a matter of resources? Or is it the basic genetics of inheritance? If it's cultural or due to resources, what it says is that societies are dramatically failing to achieve appropriate rates of social mobility, that it's the number one social problem for all societies and that President Obama is right to say that this is *the* problem his administration will tackle. If it's just a basic issue of genetics and of assortative mating with the transmission of certain types of abilities or competencies, then two things follow. The first is that we don't have a problem, and the second is that we shouldn't devote enormous resources to trying to deal with it.

DE: *Let me press you on that. One interpretation is that all that's happening is that intelligent people are passing their genes on to intelligent people and so remaining within the elite. An alternative interpretation is that there are barriers to a meritocratic society. Which is it?*

GC: My own personal bet is that genetics plays a much greater role than people have been willing to consider. One test would be this: in cultural explanations, your grandparents, cousins, and other relatives should all have some influence on your outcomes. If you're from the Jewish community, for example, then being part of that larger community network should have significant influence on your outcomes. In a genetic interpretation, if we knew the status of your parents – the underlying status – that would be the only predictor of your outcomes. Your grandparents, and all the rest of that stuff, wouldn't matter. What's more, things like resource shocks should be relatively unimportant. Interestingly, again using Oxford and Cambridge data, we can actually test whether your parents alone matter or whether your more extended lineage matters to predicting future success. And the answer is: it's only your parents.

Another test is this: a genetic explanation would say that any elite group that only marries internally would not regress to the mean, because the genetic traits conferring high status are not being lost from that group. Again, we can test this by looking at various examples, such as Brahmins in India. And we find that in societies with a high degree of endogamy, the rate of social mobility does indeed slow down.

Another implication of the genetic explanation is that any elite ethnic minority must have been selected from the top of a larger parent population by some mechanism. Again we can test this by looking at history: Ashkenazi Jews are an elite; Sephardic Jews are an elite. Are they a subset of a larger population? And the answer overwhelmingly is 'yes'. Only a small fraction of the original Jewish population has survived as Jewish. The rest converted to Christianity. And there's very strong evidence that those who remained Jewish were the elite share of the Jewish population.

We can also see that in modern America new social elites are being formed by immigration policy. People coming from areas distant from the US, without familial connections to the US, are being drawn from very high-level elites in those societies. So now, the super-elites in the US are Coptic Christians, Indian Hindus, Iranian Muslims, Maronites. And when you look across those groups, what you see is – culturally – an incredible diversity. The only group that is not represented now in the modern US elites are Protestant Anglo-Saxons! So it seems to me that what you see when you look at this data is that eliteness has nothing inherently to do with culture; it's to do with the familial transmission of abilities.

DE: *Is that one reason why your research, which has received a lot of publicity, has been given a rather pessimistic spin?*

GC: Yes, absolutely. And it's puzzling to me, firstly, why there's a universal assumption that the good society would have to have a high rate of social mobility. And, secondly, that it's a dismal discovery that genetics could actually predict what people's outcomes are going to be. Because it seems to me that in a truly meritocratic society, with universal support for everyone, the only thing left to explain differences would be genetics. And so my research is saying you're much closer to the good society than you thought.

DE: *So people have been rather depressed by your results. But you're saying they should be comforted?*

GC: Yes! I actually take it as a sign that we live in a surprisingly fair and meritocratic world.

DE: *If your interpretation of your own findings is correct, the biggest policy implication might be that governments around the world are wasting their time and money investing in trying to make society more meritocratic.*

GC: In my book on names I don't give any evidence that a whole set of individual programmes that governments are attempting are not worthwhile. But the evidence is that that would make a very small difference to the overall rate of social mobility. The evidence is that the dream of a society where every generation is born anew is a hopeless endeavour. Instead, what we have to think about is this: how do we want to organise a society where there is strong predictability from lineage — in particular, how much inequality do we want to allow in outcomes?

I take my empirical evidence as support for a very Rawlsian interpretation of social order. Our fate in life is largely determined by lineage and, in a world like that, we have to be modest about our own contributions to these outcomes and realise that it would be very wrong to excessively reward those who have the right lineage and penalise those who don't.

Societies can take radically different approaches to how they reward contributions. Compare Sweden with the United States, for example — Sweden is a much better society on that basis. Now what we're learning is that, given the realities of social mobility, the Swedish vision of social order is going to be even more appealing than the American, which relies on the idea of universal and rapid social mobility.

DE: *Do you see it as part of your role to articulate policy implications from your findings and to make normative judgements? Or are you just crunching the numbers?*

GC: I'm mainly interested in the description of the social world, and in some sense, in the physics of the social world. But, of course, one of the interesting things about doing social sciences is how closely related it is to our thinking about how we should order the world.

DE: *It sounds like you see yourself more as a scientist than a social scientist.*

GC: One of the disappointing things about economics is how little we've been able to do that has any real flavour of science. Economics is an enormously ideologically dominated subject. We have almost no laws that are either not trivial or instantly falsified. One of the astonishing things here was to discover with surnames that underlying what seems to be a very complex social world, there's a very simple social physics. And a physics that allows me, in cases like England, to make predictions two hundred years into the future about what the relative social status of groups will be. So I have drawn great comfort from the idea that even in economics we will sometimes find powerful and simple regularities that make surprising and testable predictions. I take this as a sign that, in the end, there will be no distinction between physical science and social science and that these things are much more closely aligned than we thought.

DE: *Are the ideas of testability, of falsifiability, of predictability, crucial to the robustness of your claims?*

GC: Absolutely. We're not saying anything until we're making predictions about the social world. Part of the research, in fact, conducts tests of the predicted status of people compared to their great-great-grandfathers. Then we have our model. And now we're collecting data where we test further to see how close we got, in terms of the model. I absolutely buy into the idea that to do any systematic, scientific investigation of society is to be able to make predictions.

FURTHER READING

Gregory Clark, *A Farewell to Alms: A Brief Economic History of the World* (Princeton University Press, 2007)

Gregory Clark, *The Son Also Rises: Surnames and the History of Social Mobility* (Princeton University Press, 2014)

Gregory Cochran and Henry Harpending, *The 10,000 Year Explosion: How Civilization Accelerated Human Evolution* (Basic Books, 2009)

Nicholas Wade, *A Troublesome Inheritance: Genes, Race and Human History* (Penguin, 2014)

11

ROBIN DUNBAR ON DUNBAR NUMBERS

 Robin Dunbar is Professor of Evolutionary Psychology at the University of Oxford, and a Fellow of the British Academy. His research interests lie in the evolution of sociality, with particular reference to ungulates, primates, and humans. He has been particularly interested in the structure and dynamics of human social networks and their implications for community cohesion.

David Edmonds: *How many close friends do you have? How many friends, more loosely defined, do you have? How many acquaintances do you have? How many other people can you remember? According to Robin Dunbar, most people are likely to give similar answers to these questions, and that has important implications for how humans should arrange their organisations and institutions.*

Nigel Warburton: *The topic we're focusing on is Dunbar numbers. It's unusual to have a number named after you! What is a Dunbar number?*

Robin Dunbar: Well, essentially it's the number of people that you can have a meaningful relationship with. That number is in effect a limit set by your ability to handle relationships.

NW: *We're talking about relationships at any one period, not serially?*

RD: That's right. It's the number of juggling balls you can keep in the air at the same time. But it extends to all the people with whom you have had some kind of historical relationship. Your inner core would be the ones you see regularly week by week. But if you include all the people that you might send Christmas cards to, for example, or might see or make an effort to contact at least once a year, let's say, it comes to about 150 people.

NW: *Are you suggesting there's something universal here?*

RD: Yes. As far as we can see, this is universal. We don't know much about personal social networks in other cultures, because the data we have is basically European. But there's lots of data on organisation sizes in traditional human societies which points at the same number. If you look, for example, at community size in human hunter-gatherers, these dispersed communities obviously covered a very large territory, but that number was, typically, about 150. If you look at the average village size in England and Wales in the Domesday Book, county by county, the average is about 150 again.

NW: *Obviously it's not by chance that that number, 150, has been hit upon. What's going on there?*

RD: Well, this number seems to have been pretty fixed within our species as a whole, in the last couple of hundred-thousand years. There seem to be two major possibilities. One is it's a defence against the guys over the hill, so this is the raiding-neighbour's problem. You're in an arms race, as it were, in historical terms. If you're too small you get swamped and beaten up, and so on. So there's a pressure to produce group sizes as large as you can. The other possibility is it's about trading relationships, particularly at high latitudes where things are much more unstable climatically. Therefore, food-wise, it's good to have an extended trading network, so you can go and knock on the door of the guys three valleys along and say: 'Can we come and camp with you for a bit, because remember, ten years ago, we let you come and camp with us?' So having those extended trading networks seems to have been very important in the course of later human evolution.

NW: *But in both those cases, surely a much larger number would be better?*

RD: OK. But here you get the other side of the constraint. It costs brainpower to manage groups of this size. Yes, in principle the bigger the grouping the better off you're going to be, whichever of those explanations is right. But to support those groups you need a comparably bigger brain, and that's very costly. And it turns out that at the level of the individual, the number of friends you have correlates with the size of the orbitofrontal cortex, the part of the brain just above the eyes. In other words, Dunbar number applies not only between species, where it originally came from, but also within species, between individuals.

NW: *Are you suggesting that for an individual the larger brain allows them to have a larger group of friends, or rather that dealing with friendships enlarges the brain?*

RD: That's a very interesting question, because it could be either. Given that the original predicted number of 150 is off the back of a comparative, cross-species equation showing that a species' average group-size is directly related to the size of its neocortex (essentially, the smart part of the brain), one has to suppose that there's some genetics buried in there somewhere, determining in broad terms the size and connectivity of your brain. However, we also know that the brain is quite plastic. Your experiences during development can have a significant effect on the development of particular bits of the brain. So we think that your experiences in childhood, particularly the size of your sib-ship group (the number of siblings you have), or perhaps the number of peers you play with when you're very young, can lead to the development of a slightly bigger brain than average. I've no doubt that some people just have slightly smaller brains than others, genetically, but there's some leeway there, which leads to quite large individual differences. We talk about 150 as being 'the number', but actually the number is somewhere between, let's say, 100 and 200.

And we know what causes that. It's essentially your ability to manage other people's mind-states, and that's what is determined by the size of the relevant bit of the brain. The hardware determines the software, which is this mentalising ability. How good you are at mentalising determines the number of relationships you can manage and keep going. And what's interesting in this context is that the 150 is then an emergent property, because you're not necessarily managing all those relationships individually, one by one. What you are managing is the inner core, and if you can get that right, that acts as a kind of superstructure to support the 150.

NW: *You mentioned inter-species comparisons, but if you're talking about mentalising, there are relatively few animals that could plausibly be said to have a theory of mind, or to be able to think about how another member of their species is likely to react to them.*

RD: That's certainly true. The general assumption is that most animals are operating in what's referred to as 'first-order intentionality'. They understand their own mindset; they believe that something is the case. The great apes can probably do second order, which is formal theory of mind, as the philosophers call it. That's what five-year-old children can do. In contrast, adults do much better than that: our data suggest that the average for adults is about fifth order. You're handling four other people's mind-states. It's that capacity to operate at third order, fourth order, fifth order, or sixth order as an individual that seems to be critical in determining the number of more intimate circles of friendship that you can maintain, which in turn supports the whole superstructure. But the difference between fifth order and second order, where the great apes are, is exactly the difference between having groups of 150 in humans, and groups of 50 in chimpanzees. These orders of intentionality seem to give us nice insights into human behaviour, but it seems that the bottom end of the distribution doesn't differentiate clearly enough between finer gradations within first-order intentionality so as to allow us to differentiate between the cognitive abilities of different animal species. If we knew enough about the cognitive abilities that give rise to theory of mind, we would likely be able to differentiate levels of cognitive evolution in other species.

NW: *Assuming you are right, and the number is right, does anything follow from that? It's interesting to learn something about the human species and the number of friends we can maintain. But so what?*

RD: Well, I suspect it has many implications for organisations. The classic case is the military. All modern armies are structured along these lines. This layer of 150 friends that you have turns out to consist of a series of layers, which are scaled very tightly with respect to each other. Each layer is three times bigger than the one inside it. So you have an inner, inner core of intimate friends and relations, of about five, and then there's the next layer out, that's about 15. Think of those 15 as best friends, perhaps; they're the people you might have most of your social Saturday evening barbecues with, and that number of course, includes the five. The next layer out is 50 (you might think of those as good friends), and then the 150, your friends. And we know there are at least two more layers beyond that: one at 500 which you might think of as acquaintances; again this is including everybody within the 150 as well. Finally, there's a layer at 1500, which is basically the number of faces you can put names to.

Now, you see those numbers replicated beautifully across modern armies. That's how they're structured, and they continue the series – 5000, 15,000, 50,000. So these numbers seem to work particularly effectively in terms of organisation. Remember, these layers are about the intensity of the relationship. We could think about that in terms of emotional closeness, but it probably has a lot to do with how well you understand how the other person ticks.

If you want to have an organisational unit that involves very, very close working together, you cannot do it with a group of 150: you may have to have just 15, because that's the limit, at that level of intimacy, only that number of people can work together. You can think of all sorts of knock-on consequences; instead of having secondary schools of about 1500, as we do at the moment, perhaps they should be 150 – or at least large schools that are formally subdivided into smaller units of 150 – and then they would be much more intimate.

NW: *So if people believe you, there should be some quite radical implications for some huge organisations.*

RD: Oh yes. For example, having super-ministries in Whitehall, which was a fashion at one time in the government, must have been a disaster. Think small!

NW: *You've been arguing that organisations should be relatively small, up to 150 roughly. Is there any actual evidence that they function better at that size?*

RD: There is a lot of casual evidence, though not necessarily for the group of 150, because I don't think that anybody has looked at organisations of that size in this sort of way. But, for example, this grouping layer of 15 turns out to be extremely characteristic of lots of things, such as team sports. Team members need a close understanding: you've got to know that when Jim kicks the ball he's going to place it right there, so that you can get there ahead of it. To do that, you've got to have a certain empathy between the players. And you see the same number in lots of other contexts, such as the size of juries. Why are they 12 – a number close to the 15 layer? The size of almost all inner cabinets around the world is somewhere in the order of 12 to 15. People seem to settle at these grouping layers quite naturally, according to the task they're doing.

The reasons why we might want to think of units of 150 in terms of organisational structures is essentially the same reason that the military have locked onto, and they provide probably the best example of the larger-scale unit. The smallest unit that can stand on its own two feet in modern armies is the company, which has a range in size of about 120 to 180 around the world – all modern armies fall within that span. Companies feel like family – people who have been in the military will tell you that: the company is your entire world. The battalion isn't; the other companies in the battalion are the guys you play needle matches against. They're much more needle matches, than, say, games against another branch of the military. There's something about the level of bonding and intimacy that occurs, with its limit at about 150, which seems to be crucial to how well a group of this kind functions.

And extrapolating from that, one might think in terms of schools having that kind of size, or at least being partitioned up into semi-independent sub-units of that size. That's the size in which you feel you are part of a community, and that sense of belonging actually pulls you along; you don't get left behind in a corner to fall through the cracks in the floorboard. That size has the sense of an extended family... indeed, in small-scale traditional societies that would be the typical size of your extended family.

NW: *We've now moved into the internet age and we have connections that we call 'friends' in some contexts. On Facebook or Twitter, those numbers can go a lot higher than 200. Is it that we're changing, or that those aren't really manageable friendships?*

RD: In fact, the average number of friends on Facebook is somewhere between 150 and 250. Yes, some people do have 400 or 500, but it's a very skewed distribution with a long tail. Indeed, some people have 5,000, because that's what you're allowed to have, but they're very, very few in number, and they tend to be professional users – journalists using contacts, for example, as an information source. For everyday users, you can see this huge peak of around 200. People have pretty much the same friends on Facebook as they have in everyday life, with a little slippage over into the next layer out. In fact, all you are doing when you add more friends, as Facebook prompts you to do – to befriend a friend of a friend – is adding the acquaintances layer from everyday life that runs out beyond the 150 to around 500.

What the technology does is something rather different, but still useful. It allows you to keep up with friends who are physically distant or perhaps to meet a small number of people you wouldn't normally have the chance to meet. But all our research suggests that, at the end of the day, you have to see the whites of the eyes, particularly with friends. Friendships decay with time, whereas family relationships don't. Friendships decay when you don't see the people, and they decay quite fast. What Facebook seems to do is slow down the natural rate of decay. But if you don't at some point get together over a cup of coffee, and stare into each other's eyes, my guess is there is nothing on Earth that will prevent the relationship eventually bouncing down through the layers, and dropping off the 150.

NW: *You've drawn on a number of different disciplines in what we've discussed so far; obviously evolutionary biology, but also probably sociology, psychology, philosophy and theories of mind. Do you see yourself as a social scientist?*

RD: One of these days I shall discover what I actually do. This is why I oscillate around biology, psychology, and the anthropology departments. It seems that I have moved every seven years, basically because I can't figure out which one I actually belong to. And I always blame this on the fact that my original home discipline, the degree I went to do in the first instance, and the only thing I was ever interested in at that age, was philosophy. What I learnt from philosophy was to ignore everybody else's disciplinary boundaries, and skate gracefully over them, even if they all get very upset.

FURTHER READING

Robin Dunbar, *How Many Friends Does One Person Need? Dunbar's Number and Other Evolutionary Quirks* (Faber, 2010)
Robin Dunbar, 'Instant Expert #21: Evolution of social networks', *New Scientist*, 214 (2012)
Nicholas Christakis and James H. Fowler, *Connected: The Amazing Power of our Social Networks and How They Shape Our Lives* (Harper, 2011)

12

DAViD GOLDBLATT ON THE SOCiOLOGY OF FOOTBALL

 David Goldblatt was born in London in 1965. He started a medical degree but finished with a PhD in sociology. By way of globalisation he alighted on football and in 2006 published *The Ball is Round: A Global History of Football*. Since then he has been writing, teaching, and broadcasting about sport and society. His most recent book is *The Game of Our Lives: The Making and the Meaning of English Football*.

Nigel Warburton: *Football – soccer if you prefer – is a global sport, the beautiful game. But is it really a suitable area of study for a social scientist? And could attending football matches be part of your research? Yes. Emphatically yes, says David Goldblatt, a sociologist, journalist, and author of several books on football, including* The Ball is Round.

David Edmonds: *The topic we're focusing on is the sociology of football. Sounds like a trivial subject!*

David Goldblatt: Well, it's only a trivial subject if you've not been on the planet for the last 30 years. Take the World Cup finals: no event has a larger television audience, such extraordinary international reach. Even the Olympics can't match the viewing of the World Cup. In a globalised world, here's the single most global event. A lot of the people who think football is a trivial subject are making a category mistake. Usually what they're saying is 'I don't find watching football interesting, therefore I don't find it an interesting area of study.' But it doesn't matter whether people find the game of football itself interesting. The point is that no other human behaviour can gather these kinds of crowds. And if you're a sociologist, and you're interested in the origins and consequences of collective action, you really can't beat that.

DE: *So what is the sociology of football?*

DG: Broadly speaking, I understand sociology as a discipline that starts from what actors think they're doing when they're acting, and then reflects on the unacknowledged origins and consequences of those actions. I was at a stadium in Belgrade in 2003. It was derby day: Red Star of Belgrade versus Partisan Belgrade, and Red Star were 3–0 up – at which point the Partisan fans set fire to the stadium. Now, if this were happening in England, France, or Germany, the fire engines would arrive and the football would stop. But I was the only person in the stadium saying 'What's happening? Why are we not stopping?' Everybody else just watched the football to its conclusion and indeed the police, in an extraordinary theatrical display, marched around the edge of the stadium like something out of a Busby Berkeley movie, lined up in front of the Partisan fans and their burning stand, and systematically cleared it while the second-half was played. I turned to my Serbian guide and said 'What is going on here?' And he looked at me as though I were a fool and didn't understand anything. Then he shrugged his shoulders and said 'Old Serb proverb: He who loses has the right to be angry.' Now, as a sociologist I find that extraordinary. What's going on? Why do that at football? How come the authorities are prepared to allow this to happen? What are the meanings and power relations that create an event like that?

DE: *So we should see the sociology of football as the deconstruction of norms of football-related behaviour: is that right?*

DG: Well, sometimes it's about deconstructing the norms of behaviour. But the range of topics that football offers up go way beyond mere norms, or the traditional stuff of sociology. First and foremost, football is now a very considerable industry, worth many billions of dollars, and certainly significant enough to be worth studying in its own right. And it has its own, very peculiar, economics, because this is a market-driven commercial sector where few of the people in charge are interested in making a profit: they're actually interested in winning football games. So what's going on there?

Then I'm interested in football from a geographic perspective. Look at the nature of professional football clubs. In most countries, you'll see some really interesting geographical features. For example, in Argentina, 75% of the top division comes from Buenos Aires; whereas in England, London has perhaps a quarter of the Premiership, and in other countries it may be just one or two from the capital city. This is telling us something about the degree of centralisation in these countries. In Italy, we find that the industrialised north has the richest, biggest, most powerful clubs and wins everything, and the south, traditionally more agrarian, more backward, more isolated and marginal, wins nothing. And these facts are not unrelated; one can link the geography to the economy and to the sport. Of course, as Sven-Göran Eriksson, the Swedish manager of England in the early 2000s, said, there is more politics in football than in politics, and he's not wrong. At the international level, FIFA is notorious as an international organisation, one which is far better known, I would say, than almost any other, more even than the IMF or World Bank, and whose dealings are closely followed all over the world. It's clearly a highly political organisation both in terms of its internal politics, but also in its relationships with nation states, national football associations, and so on.

DE: *You've talked about organisations, the clubs, and you've talked about football as an industry. But presumably football is a subject that lends itself to other sociological angles – for example, the study of crowd behaviour and the role of ethnicity in football.*

DG: Yes. If you're interested in collective action and the sociology of the crowd, football is perfect. Football chanting, for example, dramatises one of the most interesting and important dilemmas in sociology, which is: 'What is the relationship between agency and structure?' How do individuals combine together collectively to produce different results? How come crowds sing spontaneously? How do they react to events the way they do?

You discover some interesting things when you actually sit in a crowd. First of all you have chant entrepreneurs, people who've got enough *chutzpah* and energy to stand up and start singing and not care whether anybody else sings line two or three. Then you'll see the people closest to them, sometimes their friends, who will join in on the second line. Then the question is, will it hit that critical intensity where you've got enough people singing the third line that everyone else is prepared to come in? And have you noticed how, with applause, it doesn't end in a random fashion but rather it starts dipping and it comes to that moment where a very large number of a crowd think, 'Oh God. I don't want to be the last person clapping,' and it all stops simultaneously? And the same goes for singing and chanting as well.

As for questions of ethnicity and gender, you couldn't ask for more from football. Football is particularly interesting because it's an arena where the politics of the body, the politics of visibility, the sociology of performance – all come together in dramatic fashion. Take the case of post-war England: what was the place in which young black men were most often seen publicly? There's no question that it's the football pitch. And so we can tell a story, not merely a metaphorical one, about the structure of feeling in post-war Britain, which looks at the experiences of that first generation of black footballers – how they were received by the crowd and how their grit and bravery and determination in the face of racist chanting was an important moment for immigrant communities here. The message was: 'We are not leaving. We are part of this and you can say what you like. We're dug in.' And this forced the crowd and the football authorities to start engaging with these issues.

This is repeated all over the world. It's not just an issue of black or white. It's an issue of religion. The experience of Palestinian Arabs, or Israeli Arabs, within Israeli football takes on this form; the experience of Poles or new African migrants to Germany; or think of Mario Balotelli, a man of West African roots, but brought up as an Italian citizen. These people are lightning rods, both for the racism that is inherent in the wider society and expressed through football crowds, as well as for opportunities to make an anti-racist case.

DE: *I want to pick up on one of the phrases you used in that answer. You said 'We can tell a story.' I wondered how important narrative is in doing what you do?*

DG: Narrative is really important to me. Sociology has a bent towards the analytical of the now. You sort out the structural relations of a moment or an event. And that's important.

But sociology is inevitably a historical discipline too, because you're always asking what the structural origins of something are, where did this stuff come from? You're never going to be able to capture the meaning of contemporary action without understanding how it is rooted in historical structures. So, for me, to do sociology is always to be doing history.

There's another important aspect to narrative. If you're interested in communicating with the wider public, and that is top of my personal agenda, then you have to do some storytelling. There are a very few people in this world who can write abstractly, theoretically, and intellectually and really engage an audience without the use of narrative. Certainly I am not up to that task. A lot of the energy, as well as the intellectual strength of the work that I do is in narrative, is in storytelling. That's a very un-academic term: it suggests triviality and entertainment, but I don't see it in that way. I think that's the prejudice of academic language, and actually a lot of the best intellectual work has a narrative quality to it.

So much of football culture is about narrative history. When you start supporting Arsenal, you're not just supporting the Arsenal of now, you're supporting and embracing a whole series of cultural meanings, stories of the past, which cumulatively constitute what Arsenal is. Because Arsenal is not a stadium – that can change. It's not the Board, it's not the shares or the players. All of these things can come and go. What gives it consistency across time is this accumulated fund of cultural capital – the narrative, the emotional stories invested in it. Football is completely hooked on that. Now, most of the history that is told and constructed in popular football culture is ersatz history: it's got no documentary basis, it's unchallenged, unreflective, it's desperately sentimental, it's appallingly clichéd; and it's unreferenced and unchecked. However, all of that can be remedied, and often a better story emerges from a critical sociological engagement, and one that speaks to people who might not otherwise engage with sociological ideas.

DE: *And is sociology that isn't narrative driven, and which doesn't communicate so well with a general public, bad sociology?*

DG: No, not necessarily. I use a lot of that stuff myself. I haven't been around the stadiums of the Premier League counting how many women and how many ethnic minorities are attending.

That's really important work and I don't denigrate it in any way. Someone's got to do it, and I have great respect for it when it's done well. But I often feel that in contemporary British academic culture it's slightly the be-all and end-all of life. It's just what you do, and you churn it out, and that's a shame because I think more, and better, can be done with it. But that stuff's really important. It's just going to be very under-used, which is a shame given how much time and energy is put into producing it in the first place.

DE: *So you use that academic material, and obviously football is a topic which is widely covered in the media and that must be a useful resource for you. You've already said that you yourself go to football matches. Is that part of your research too?*

DG: Yes. I'm a huge participant observer. I've been to see football in perhaps 35 countries. If comparative sociology is what floats your boat, then football, and being at the games, is perfect for doing this. Because it's the same everywhere – 90 minutes, two ends, two halves – and yet everywhere it's completely different.

DE: *And are you there taking notes?*

DG: I don't take notes because then you look like a participant observer. So no, I never take notes at games. I do it all mentally.

DE: *But are you observing aspects of the spectacle through a sociological lens?*

DG: You can't leave the sociological perspective at home. Sir Karl Popper, in his famous lectures at the LSE, held up a pencil and said 'Observe!' and then sat down. After 15 minutes one of the braver members of the class stood up and said 'Observe what?' 'Ah-ha', said Popper. And so one always goes with a purpose, with a structure. I don't show up at these things and go, 'Oh who or what am I going to see?' I've got a mental checklist of what I'm looking for. I do an instant demographic of the crowd. Is it male, is it female? What's the ethnicity? What's the age? I look at the geographical distribution around the stadium. Where are they standing? Where are they sitting? How do the hard-core fans organise themselves? How are people dressed? What emblems do people bring, what flags? What kind of choreography is going on? Do they arrive early? Do they arrive late? What is the setting of this stadium?

How do we read its architectural meaning? Who owns this football club? What are their political interests in doing so? Are they here? How do they behave when they are here? I've got a checklist of about 500 questions, and I always try to make contact with people. Before I go I've probably spent a couple of hours in the centre of town hanging out with people who run a fans group or who are the ultras (organised fan groups, first emerging in Italy in the late 1960s, best known for orchestrating pyrotechnic displays and vast stadium banners). That's how I go to the football. And I try and watch the football too.

DE: *You have to understand the language of football to mix with the supporters. You have to be a fan yourself really.*

DG: I don't think you have to be a fan. What do we mean by 'fan'? Do we mean someone who's emotionally involved in one of the two participating sides, or a fan in the sense that you like watching football? I think it would be quite hard to do if you didn't at some level like watching football. The great Uruguayan writer, Eduardo Galeano, wrote something interesting in *Football in Sun and Shadow*. He's a Peñarol supporter and their great opponents are Nacional, also based in Montevideo, and he describes a moment where he sees Nacional scoring a fantastic goal and despite himself, he loved it, he enjoyed it. He described himself as a beggar: 'I'm just a beggar for good football, from wherever it comes.' And I'm a beggar too, but I'm a beggar for other people's meanings; that's what really blows me away. Everywhere I go in this world, I find that all sorts of complex narratives and meanings are associated with the following of football. That's what's really exciting me when I'm standing in a crowd.

DE: *It sounds like a very descriptive approach to the discipline. Is there any normative element to it?*

DG: There is a normative element to it. I come at this from a pretty left-wing perspective; I don't hide that. I come at it from a perspective that thinks institutions should be democratic. I come at it always from the side of the little people. In all the fights and oppositions in football, I end up taking a position. But I think everybody regards football as political. It's not me coming along and politicising an otherwise lovely, gentle, inno-cent, apolitical game. The playing of football, the watching, the consuming, and the following of football have assumed political dimensions everywhere. Look at FIFA: their slogan is 'For the world, for the game'. We might love that and we might be cynical about it. But it's extraordinary that an international sporting body is making a claim to, in some sense, represent humanity, or be a contributor to the global common good. That is a political position. Once you start talking about the common good in the public realm, we're in the land of politics. Then we have a conversation about what is the public good? Who represents it? How does the way this game is played, watched, followed, and experienced reflect that?

DE: *And if you take a political stance, can your writings be an instrument of change?*

DG: I really hope they can be. That's what motivates me. For a long time, football, as a set of cultural institutions, has hidden its politics and its power precisely behind the arguments that deem it trivial, apolitical, just a game. What that's done is provide ideological cover for the people who run the show, and football, if nothing else, is a popular creation. Arsenal doesn't mean anything unless a lot of people think that it matters. A football game played in an empty stadium is the most miserable, meaningless experience. We have to have a popular conception of sovereignty in football politics because the meanings of this game are generated collectively, and once we're in that realm, questions of democracy, questions of the distribution of power, questions of common ownership, come into play. I hope that by demonstrating the degree of politicisation in football, and the way in which meanings are collectively produced, one can encourage the people who love the game, in all of the millions of different ways that you can love and engage with it, to grapple with the political dimension.

FURTHER READING

David Goldblatt, *The Ball is Round: A Global History of Football* (Penguin, 2006)

David Goldblatt, *The Game of Our Lives: The Making and the Meaning of English Football* (Penguin, 2014)

Richard Holt, *Sport and the British* (OUP, 2009)

Bill Buford, *Among the Thugs* (Arrow, 1992)

Simon Kuper and Stefan Syzmanski, *Why England Lose* (Harper Collins, 2010)

13

TREVOR MARCHAND ON CRAFT

Trevor Marchand is Professor of Social Anthropology at SOAS and recipient of the RAI Rivers Medal (2014). He is trained in architecture (McGill), anthropology (SOAS), and fine woodwork (Building Crafts College). Marchand has conducted fieldwork with masons and craftspeople in Yemen, Mali, and East London. He is the author of *Minaret Building and Apprenticeship in Yemen* (2001), *The Masons of Djenné* (2009), and *The Pursuit of Pleasurable Work* (forthcoming), and editor of, among others, *Making Knowledge* (2010) and *Craftwork as Problem Solving* (2016). He has produced and directed documentary films, and curated exhibitions at the RIBA and the Smithsonian Institution.

David Edmonds: *It's an unusual approach for an academic: a hands-on approach. Literally a hands-on approach. Trevor Marchand is an anthropologist interested in how information about crafts is transferred from expert to novice. This has led him to Nigeria, Yemen, Mali, and East London and has required him to use his hands to build, among other things, minarets and homes of mudbrick.*

Nigel Warburton: *The topic we're going to focus on is craft. Now, you're a social anthropologist; what is the special interest in craft?*

Trevor Marchand: Craft opens up a huge window onto the world. It is about learning, knowing, and problem solving. But craft isn't simply the making of things; it's also the consumption of hand-made objects. It involves the politics behind making things 'by hand' and the web of social relations between craftspeople, suppliers of materials, patrons, and clients. There's often a power hierarchy between them, especially in the case of apprenticeship training regimes. Gender issues, too, arise; and more so depending on the kind of craft in question. So, in sum, the study of craft is a vehicle to understanding social and cultural dynamics.

NW: *As a researcher how do you narrow that down? Because it sounds almost as if you're investigating the whole of the society when you look at craft.*

TM: I think I need to. I need to understand all of those issues and more because they form the backdrop to my real foci, which are human learning and knowledge. So, in order to understand how people learn something – how they acquire skills – I need to have an understanding of that full context because learning is situated and it's interactive. So I must know where the individual craftspeople I'm working with are coming from, and where they're positioned in society and within their community, in order to get a better grasp of how it is that they learn. Everybody learns differently.

NW: *Can you give an example of how you went about that?*

TM: I enjoy working with my hands, so developing the kind of fieldwork method that I use was quite straightforward. I have always 'signed up' during fieldwork: I usually start off on a building site as a labourer. In Mali and in Yemen, I began at that level and then I tried to work my way up to becoming an apprentice. In Mali, I succeeded in being taken on as a full apprentice. A few years later, at the Building Crafts College in East London, I registered for the full-time two-year programme in fine woodwork. A hands-on approach allows me to be immersed daily in my subject of study. So, it's a way of learning by doing.

NW: *And learning by learning.*

TM: And learning by learning, absolutely. In fact, my ultimate goal is to learn about learning.

NW: *Now, just to be clear, when you were working in Mali, for instance, you were actually working – you were researching – but at the same time you were earning a salary, presumably; you were participating as a worker in this society?*

TM: I've always foregone the salaries because I can never completely remove myself from my researching role. My fellow builders and craftspeople knew I was there as a researcher; that was made very clear from the beginning. For ethical reasons, they had to know what I was there for and what I was looking for, but that was often forgotten in the day-to-day work on the building site where I became a member of the team. My physical labour on a project and the friendship I could offer were the most valuable contributions I could make to a building team. Also, interestingly, for many of the workers I was a window onto another world: in their minds, I represented Canada, or Europe, or the West. And so, my interest in them was reciprocated by their interest in me.

NW: *One of the projects that you worked on was building minarets in Yemen. That's unusual for somebody from Canada to be doing. What was it like? What were you doing on a day-to-day basis?*

TM: I didn't expect to work on a minaret-building project when I first arrived in Yemen. I was hoping that I might be able to join a group of builders working on the restoration of a house or another small project. But it so happened that there was a minaret being built along the road where I was staying when I first arrived in Sana'a (Yemen's capital city). That provided a wonderful opportunity to just go and sit on the roadside – I literally sat on the curb each morning – to watch them building. It was fascinating. No scaffolding is used for making these towering structures: they're built from the inside out. The spiral staircase is built in tandem with the exterior wall, and the labourers relay the materials along it to the top. I would watch the masons perched on the top of the wall laying the brick courses, progressing in a counter-clockwise direction as the structure rose higher. Finally, one morning, the master mason came down and asked 'What are you doing? We see you every day.' I responded 'Well, I'm hoping to work alongside some builders. I want to understand the building processes as well as the apprentice system here.' And he said 'Why don't you come up and see our work?', inviting me to the top of the minaret. The master mason jumped from the top of the staircase onto the narrow circumference wall – at that stage of construction, it was nearly 30 metres in the air – and he looked back at me challengingly. Luckily I don't suffer vertigo, and so I leapt onto the wall after him and followed him around the perimeter of the structure.

I told him that I would love to work with him on this building and he said, 'Ahlan wa sahan, you are welcome, and you can begin tomorrow.' So I started the next morning and I worked with them for 13 months. I kept a pen and notepad in my pocket. I wore big baggy work pants with pockets to keep them in and I periodically stopped to take notes on what was going on. I was working in the stairwell most of the time with the labourers – and sometimes at the top as an apprentice with the masons. I enjoyed a privileged position because the other labourers and even the apprentices were not permitted to ask questions. It was considered to be an affront to the esteemed masters if they did. But the masons appreciated that my position was a little bit different and they tolerated my occasional questioning while working. Most of what I learned was through my direct social relations with the other builders and the tasks we performed together. In the late afternoon, when work stopped, we would get together to chew *khat* – which is a mild narcotic leaf chewed in South Arabia and parts of Africa. And that made time for reflection and for discussing issues and ideas in greater depth.

NW: *I can imagine that process reveals a wealth of detail about the practicalities of building a minaret, but presumably you're looking for generalities as well? It's not just a matter of learning the specifics.*

TM: That goes back to something I was telling you earlier: I need to have that background information in order to understand the context that gives rise to learning and enskilment. For instance, while working in Sana'a, I needed to understand gender relations and the nature of competing masculinities. I also needed to understand the growing popularity of 'traditional' architecture among urban elites and the role that craftwork continues to play in the making of the city. Interestingly, the masons don't have a guild structure like masons and crafts-people in other regions of the Middle East. I had to understand the pecking order on the building site and within the broader building-construction community; and the various building materials in terms of their properties and where they were coming from. All of that was very important. I could initially learn about some of these things from the existing literature, and then gain deeper understanding by being on site. The existing literature is where anthropologists normally develop their initial background understanding: before starting fieldwork, anthropologists investigate the regional literature, and try to understand the historic and cultural context that they will be working within. But because my particular interests are in knowledge, learning, and embodiment, I need to go that extra step to also become conversant in the kinds of physical practices and activities that I'm studying. So I need to participate in them directly in order to get that background 'bodily' understanding of what's going on, similar to the way that I need to be familiar with the subject literature. My participation gave me the background to draw upon in order to better understand what my fellow builders and craftspeople were doing, what they were experiencing, and how they were incrementally learning their trade.

NW: *What's interesting to me is that you didn't just stop with 13 months there but you immersed yourself in other craft situations at a similar depth. Presumably, patterns emerge and you can start to understand what's going on more generally with people who are working with their hands?*

TM: Yes, definitely. One of the reasons that I shifted my field site to West Africa was that I wanted to conduct a comparative study. There were some very interesting similarities; but I think perhaps even more interesting were the differences between the training systems. In Sana'a (Yemen), the masons' apprenticeship system was quite strict and disciplinarian in nature, and the apprentice didn't enjoy a fixed or stable position. If they fell out of favour, they were pushed back down the hierarchy to become a labourer again, only to be replaced by another. In Djenné (Mali), where I worked, the position of an apprentice was more secure: it usually involved a verbal contract made between the parents of the young man who was coming into the trade and the master mason, who may or may not have been a member of the extended family. The stability of their position meant that there was more tolerance for questioning and investigation on the part of the apprentices, and even the labourers. There was also a greater exchange of humour and bantering on the building sites. I would say that, in general, Djenné was a more convivial place to work. But perhaps most strikingly, masons in both places are operating within Islamic contexts, but religion manifests itself very differently in the respective masons' practices. In Mali there was an integration of what might be glossed as non-Islamic beliefs: benedictions and spells comprising a mix of Qur'anic verse and local lore played a very important role not just in people's lives but in the building process itself. The Djenné masons started each morning by making benedictions before beginning to lay bricks, and that was to 'guarantee' the safety of those working on site, as well as the future prosperity and well-being of those who would come to live there. Clients were aware of the masons' power to make these guarantees, so it was important for masons to perform their spells and benedictions in an overt fashion so that clients and members of the general public could witness them. In effect, benedictions were as important to the stability of a structure as the mortar between bricks. So, that day-to-day integration of different kinds of knowledge in the trade was in stark contrast to what I observed among the Yemeni masons, whose Islamic practices might be considered more 'orthodox'.

NW: *And presumably that was quite different from your experience of woodworking in the East End of London.*

TM: Absolutely. My next major case study was conducted among fine woodwork trainees and established furniture makers in the UK. I wanted to compare the vocational training that individuals undergo in a western European context with what I had observed in West Africa and Arabia. Among the woodworkers, for example, literacy and numeracy were necessary skills in addition to acquiring embodied ones and possessing knowledge about the properties of the materials and the specialised tools that they used. The young men and women took written exams and they were required to demonstrate an ability to calculate proportions, geometries, quantities, and costings for the set carpentry pieces they made. They problem-solved with mathematical equations. That alone was very different from the West African and Arabian contexts where many of the young men whom I worked with were illiterate and innumerate, and thus their mastery of quantities, proportion, and symmetry were examined and assessed exclusively in what they produced 'by eye' or in relation to their body.

NW: *What you're describing here is a range of different apprenticeships, a range of different approaches to learning in the craft situation. Are you attempting to view these from a neutral perspective, or through your engagement with these sub-cultures or cultures are you trying to give your research a political or moral angle?*

TM: My research has always had a political slant to it. I think of myself as a craftsperson – I'm originally an architect, and what I enjoyed most about architecture was the crafting of the drawings. I also enjoyed visiting my building sites and working alongside the carpenters to resolve problems. Documenting and analysing the various ways that craftspeople problem-solve is a key part of my research. It's important to generate among the general public a greater appreciation for the diversity of embodied skills and knowledge that goes into designing and making something. For far too many centuries, a division between manual labour and intellectual work has persisted. Leonardo da Vinci made that distinction between manual labour and intellectual work, reflected in the division made between 'craftwork' and 'fine art'. Unfortunately, vocational education – not just here in the UK but in other parts of the world – is something that children go into, or are steered into, when their peers or parents judge that they're not academically gifted; working with the hands is perceived as a fallback position – a second choice. So, by challenging the mind–body dichotomy, my research aims to explore and expose the complexity of knowledge that is actually involved in handwork, and thereby raise its status in the eyes of educationalists, the government, and the general public.

NW: *From your experience of a range of different apprenticeship situations, which is the best one?*

TM: I don't think I'd impose any hierarchy on them. They're all very different, and I enjoyed working in all three contexts immensely. But, in some ways, the vocational education that we're offering young people here (in the UK) is weaker than other apprenticeships. Apprenticeships in Arabia and Africa didn't merely involve learning the skills to put up buildings: apprentices also learned general site management. On a daily basis, they were exposed to the conversations between their masters and the suppliers of building materials, or the financial negotiations with clients. They were also instructed in the moral comportment necessary for a craftsperson to become a success. The minaret builders in Yemen knew that it was important for masons to be seen praying on a regular basis, and to observe the fast during Ramadan. Demonstrations of piety resulted in greater trust from clients, and thus contracts. Likewise, in Djenné, the work was not simply a matter of putting up buildings: it was about learning the benedictions to make buildings stand – a master only passed that knowledge on to the apprentices with whom he had established close relationships, whom he trusted, and whom he believed had developed a deep understanding of things.

The curriculum in the London vocational college also included 'moral' instruction. Good conduct was conveyed by the instructors: I have been privileged to work with people who are absolutely outstanding at inculcating a sense of responsibility in their trainees toward future clients and working within budgets, and so on. But the experience of real, everyday business interactions and transactions was missing from the college setting. This is a serious problem because many of the trainees who come straight out of college find it very difficult to set up on their own despite that being their principal aspiration. The traditional apprentice, working and learning on site, by contrast, finds it easier to move along because they've already got experience of the business skills, social skills, and comportment necessary for running their own business.

NW: *Surely it's a feature of the modern world that the many things that were formerly done by hand are now done by machine. So, in a way, we're moving away from the world of craft, aren't we?*

TM: The question that you ask is not new. Thomas Carlyle, John Ruskin, William Morris, and others ever since were very much interested in that same question. I actually don't believe that craft as an idea, or a concept, would exist without mass production and industrialisation. Craft's identity is constructed through its differentiation from those modes of production. In fact, I would say that the fascination with handicraft has been strong and steady across the past two centuries. That fascination is not just in the things hand-made but in the social politics behind that mode of production. This intrigue has increased during the past few decades, compounded with green issues and questions about sustainability. Growing numbers of consumers are interested in things with a story, and what better story is there than knowing exactly where the materials came from, who the maker was, and how the object was made? A fundamental reason why people continue going into handwork/craftwork is to reestablish a connection between themselves and their livelihoods: a connection between maker and the materials they're working with; the tools they're gripping in their hands; and, hopefully, the market that they sell to – and perhaps even the landscape in which they practise.

It all goes back to Marx's notion of alienation, and the desire to pursue a livelihood that challenges contemporary forms of alienation. This isn't a phenomenon exclusive to the West. The situation in Djenné, for instance, is similar in interesting ways. Djenné was made a UNESCO World Heritage Site in 1988. That designation dragged the entire urban fabric into contested territory. Who owns the town's architectural heritage? Does it belong to the 'world' – whatever that means? Is it something for UNESCO to oversee? Does it any longer belong to the local population? And this has impacted the status and position of the craftspeople who continue to erect Djenné's buildings, and it has placed limitations on their practice. In many respects, they are expected to reproduce the kind of traditional architecture that existed when Djenné was declared a UNESCO World Heritage Site. That limits their potential for innovating and for responding more directly to the changing needs and aesthetic tastes of clients. What they're producing, in a certain sense, has become a commodity for a global tourist economy.

NW: *Has your research on learning and how we learn changed your attitude to learning?*

TM: Yes. One of the things I learned first-hand on site – on the building sites as well as the trade college – is that you're not always going to get the easy answers that you're looking for from your mentors and instructors. Some of the very best are those who turn trainees' questions into another question – a very Socratic approach to education. This results in individuals who can think for themselves. This is something I have tried to emulate in both my teaching of undergraduate students and my supervision of PhD students. I want my students to own their questions and their pursuits of knowledge. I want them to own their projects. I'm there as scaffolding, but at the end of the day their real pleasure will come from their own discovery of answers, solutions, or just simply 'a way forward'. So, that spirit is something that I've taken away from my field studies.

NW: *I can't believe that working for so long with your hands hasn't in some way led you away from academia, because it's such a different style of living from the typical academic.*

TM: I've always felt torn. I've always thought of myself as a maker and it's probably still my greatest pleasure; it's where I really lose myself, just being completely absorbed in designing and making something. When I moved from architecture into anthropology, it was to address a set of theoretical questions that I knew would be best addressed by pursuing a PhD in anthropology, though at that time I was still designing houses. Since then I've moved out of the architectural profession – mostly – and I try to strike a balance between my academic work and a hands-on involvement in making things for myself. But I very much look forward to a time where the balance tips once again in favour of the making.

FURTHER READING

Trevor H.J. Marchand (ed.), *Craftwork as Problem Solving* (Ashgate Publishing, 2016)

Trevor H.J. Marchand, 'Knowledge in Hand: Explorations of brain, hand and tool', in Richard Fardon, Olivia Harris and Trevor Marchand et al. (eds), *The Sage Handbook of Social Anthropology*, volume 2, pp. 261–272 (Sage, 2012)

Trevor H.J. Marchand, *The Masons of Djenné* (Indiana University Press, 2009)

Michael Herzfeld, *The Body Impolitic: Artisans and Artifice in the Global Hierarchy of Value* (University of Chicago Press, 2004)

Tim Ingold, *The Perception of the Environment: Essays on Livelihood, Dwelling and Skill* (Routledge, 2000)

14

BRUCE HOOD ON
THE SUPERNATURAL

Bruce Hood is the Director of the Bristol Cognitive Development Centre in the Experimental Psychology Department at the University of Bristol. He undertook his PhD at Cambridge University followed by appointments at University College London, MIT, and as a faculty professor at Harvard. He has been awarded an Alfred Sloan Fellowship in neuroscience, the Young Investigator Award from the International Society of Infancy Researchers, the Robert Fantz Memorial Award, and the Media and Public Engagement Award by the British Psychological Society. He is a Fellow of the American Psychological Society, the Royal Institution of Great Britain, the Royal Society of Biology, and the British Psychological Society. He is the President of the British Association for Science psychology section. He was the Royal Institution Christmas Lecturer in 2011 and has written three popular science books, *SuperSense: Why We Believe the Unbelievable* (2009), *The Self Illusion: Why There is No 'You' Inside Your Head* (2012), and *The Domesticated Brain* (2014). He is the founder of Speakezee.org – the world's largest academic speaker website.

David Edmonds: *You may believe that you are immune to supernatural attitudes or beliefs: they're for others, for more primitive, more superstitious types. But Bruce Hood, a developmental psychologist at the University of Bristol, says supernatural beliefs are much more common than you think. You've probably got some.*

Nigel   *The topic we're going to focus on is the supernatural. Now that seems*
Warburton: *a very strange subject for a reputable scientist to be investigating.*
                   Could you say something about that?

Bruce   Yes, well, I have to confess I got into psychology under false
Hood: pretences. When I was a young boy I'd watch Uri Geller doing
                   these amazing things and I really did believe there must be
                   something to it because everyone was saying he had all these
                   abilities. So I wanted to study psychology to learn how to use
                   my mind to control the physical world and all that sort of
                   nonsense. I very soon discovered that there's no credible
                   evidence for the supernatural, or 'paranormal' as it was called
                   at the time. Instead, I discovered there's a much more fasci-
                   nating area of empirical work on the mind, and I particularly
                   focused on child development.

                   Many decades passed, and then when I arrived in Bristol about
                   15 years ago I set up a laboratory to study child development.
                   I'd never really abandoned my interest and fascination with
                   the supernatural. Rather than considering it a plausible phe-
                   nomenon in its own terms, I became more interested in why
                   people believe in it. In my studies on children I noticed that
                   there were many misconceptions that they came up with.
                   Along with other psychologists, I recognised that you could
                   see the basis of adult supernatural thinking emerging natu-
                   rally in the way that children reason about the world. So I
                   became fascinated with the natural way of understanding the
                   world and how that could lay down the foundations of super-
                   natural thinking.

NW: *That's really interesting. So you're saying that young children are*
                   already forming patterns of behaviour and belief that tend them
                   towards a kind of supernatural explanation in later life?

BH: Yes, effectively. The premise is that the brain is a sophisticated
                   pattern-recognising system: we generate explanations to make
                   sense of the patterns that we discover in the world. So when
                   we see two events happening close in time the tendency is to
                   think that one causes the other. You have a thought about
                   someone that you haven't thought about for a long time, then
                   you get a phone call out of the blue: the immediate assumption
                   is that you somehow have some psychic connection, when

in fact you've probably forgotten every instance where you've been thinking about someone and no one has contacted you. So we pick up on what we perceive as being significant events and we interpret them as some sort of causal effect. Take for example, pareidolia; this is this tendency to see faces in objects in the world.

We know that the brain has systems for recognising face-like structures, and in fact that's wired into the newborn's brain – there are studies of newborns showing that they prefer to look at patterns which look like faces. So we are very good at finding face-like patterns. Or think about energies and forces, the assumption that some things have a hidden property. My particular research interest is a field known as essentialism. This is the attribution of a hidden dimension to things which somehow gives them their true identity. It's almost as if there's a sort of spiritual component. When you start to think about essentialism you can see it operating everywhere, not only in supernatural thinking, but also in the way that we think about what makes things irreplaceable. So I'm fascinated by this sort of crossover between natural reasoning and then this sort of emergence of supernatural assumptions.

NW: *Let's take that concept of essentialism. I have an object with senti-mental value – I own a baton that my grandfather used to conduct an orchestra with. Now, that's got sentimental value. It's not replaceable by another baton that looks just the same. It seems to have some essential almost magical quality because it was his baton. Is that the kind of thing you're talking about?*

BH: Yes, that's it. The example I usually give is a wedding ring. I say to people 'This is your wedding ring, would you be happy to swap it for an identical wedding ring?' Most people if they're enjoying a happy marriage will say 'No'. Then you say 'Why not?' and they say 'Well, because it's not the original.' But the trouble with things being original is that there are some metaphysical issues about what constitutes an original item.

For example, from philosophy, we know the problem of the Ship of Theseus. I'll give a brief summary of it. This is a story of a ship belonging to Theseus which was put into storage. Over the years the shipwrights would come back and they had to replace some of the planks. Eventually they replaced all the planks. The question is, was this still the original Ship of Theseus? You might say 'Well yes, it's a gradual replacement.' But then if you reassembled all the original rotting planks that were put into storage you'd now have two ships. Which then would be the original Ship of Theseus?

Our intuition is that gradual transformations retain identity. Sudden rapid transformations – when the object becomes something completely different – don't. We tend to think there's something beyond the material composition which gives objects their identity, and this is what I call the *essence* of the object. The research on children's essentialism is really to do with living things. But now I think we're beginning to recognise that this also applies to objects to which you have an emotional connection. So this is the origin of essentialism.

NW: *Could it be that the fundamental starting point for essentialism is other people, since they obviously change significantly over time?*

BH: Absolutely. That's my hunch. When we form emotional attachments to significant others then we essentialise them. We think there's a property which makes them irreplaceable. For example, we don't form these attachments to polystyrene cups or things which are clearly duplicated. It also explains why I think that we find identical twins rather alarming, or the notion of genetic modification almost an assault on the essence of what gives something it's true identity. So we hold deep-seated beliefs about retaining authenticity and true identity. It's the same with works of art. As soon as you discover a work of art isn't by who you thought it was, it loses not only financial value, but some of our emotional attachment to it.

NW: *Are you saying that this is magical thinking? Because it seems quite normal thinking. If you are, then we are all engaging in magical thinking some of the time.*

BH: Absolutely. It becomes manifest in daily practices, the way that we buy certain products which we feel are irreplaceable. There's a whole industry of foods that we eat which we think will imbue us with special powers. You have Chinese medicine which includes the assumption that if you eat certain animal parts you will retain or gain some of the power that is stored in it. There's a lot of this going on all the time. Now it sounds like it's irrational, but it's not necessarily irrational. There's a whole line of research which explains why we might be essentialists, which is that we try to avoid contamination. This comes from the field of disgust. But yes, what I'm saying is that this way of inferring a deeper dimension and visible properties of things is very commonplace and it manifests sometimes as supernatural thinking, but also manifests in our evaluation of what makes something unique.

NW: *How can you tease apart the aspects which are magical from the aspects which just happen to make people unique or other things unique?*

BH: Sometimes they will say there's an essence in there or they'll say that this has got a certain vibe. So they might articulate a belief for which there's no scientific evidence. But more often than not what we do in our studies is look for behaviours which suggest that they are relying on this assumption. So, for example, I did a study some years ago asking people if they'd be willing to wear a cardigan. I offered them an incentive of £20. Most people would. But then you say 'Actually, would you still wear it if you knew it belonged to the serial killer Fred West?' Most people would decline. When you say 'Well, why wouldn't you wear it?', some people say 'I don't want to be seen to be someone who's willing to wear Fred West's cardigan.' But that just restates the problem. What's wrong with wearing a killer's cardigan? Others will say 'It feels disgusting. It feels dirty.' It's almost as if they're applying a biological explanation.

We're now actually doing work where we get people to put on or touch clothing and then we inform them that it belongs to someone very good or someone very evil. We then watch what happens next. Do they wash their hands? Do they try and get clean of contamination? That would suggest that they are acting irrationally. But there's a good reason why they might behave like this. We don't know why people are crazed killers. There *might* be a biological contamination. So in that sense it's not an entirely irrational response. But when you explain this, people say 'Well, I know it's a bit strange, but it just makes me feel yucky.' So that's what I mean by supernatural thinking because if these things were real, if these dimensions and forces and energies were real, they wouldn't be supernatural: they'd be natural.

NW: *So there's no significant molecular change brought about by Fred West wearing a cardigan – presumably it's been washed anyway. And in your experiments the cardigan wasn't really Fred West's, but just the thought that it was his was enough to make people feel revulsion?*

BH: Yes, that's exactly it. It's what you think something is which will affect your behaviour. So for example, we conducted a study asking people to cut up photographs of sentimental objects or photographs of their wives. We found that even though they knew these were just photographs, they exhibited significant increases in stress. Systems in the brain are triggered by irrational supernatural intuitions, but you can suppress them or control them by top-down logical analysis. But they're always in conflict. And there are no atheists in the foxhole, or at 30,000 feet when the plane hits turbulence. Any of us can revert to this sort of magical thinking.

NW: *You moved quite quickly from talking about magical thinking to talking about religious belief. For a lot of people those are quite distinct areas.*

BH: Yes. It's funny isn't it, that they should draw that distinction?! But of course religion is just organised supernatural thinking. Every religion has to have entities with supernatural powers. I think part of that works because of the pull of the supernatural: there's something that transcends the mundane and so it has to have supernatural qualities. Religions are just organised narratives about the beginnings of the universe, the end of the universe, and why we're on this planet, where we go when we're dead. They're just stories to some extent, but are punctuated with and require these belief systems; whereas people can be non-religious and yet still believe in a whole variety of supernatural things. So I think the difference is this: religion is organised supernatural thinking; supernatural thinking also occurs spontaneously in other belief systems.

NW: *Are these patterns of thinking learned through early conditioning? Or are they, perhaps, the result of innate patterns of thought and action we evolved in the Pleistocene?*

BH: As in so many areas of psychology, it's a combination of the two. There are predispositions that actually explain why one brother will become very religious and the other one might become an ardent atheist. There's always variation. The studies which have looked for the shared likelihood of these, for example twin studies, do support the idea that there's some genetic basis for it. So my suggestion is that we're pre-wired to see structured order and to infer causes. Whether these tendencies emerge as full-blown supernatural religious ideas really depends on the culture in which you're raised.

NW: *It's not hard to see that there are people who visit psychics and clairvoyants and sincerely believe what they're told. But there are many who think of themselves as rational, and are, perhaps, scientists themselves. It's hard to believe that they're caught up in this.*

BH: That's true. But often people have beliefs which are supernatural without realising they're supernatural. The common one I point to is the belief that you can tell when you're being watched from behind. Nine out of ten people think they can do that, but they can't. There are many common assumptions that we never challenge because they seem intuitively correct. If you're facing a time of threat then people will typically clutch at anything which gives them some sense of control. Many superstitious behaviours or rituals are attempts to control uncontrollable events. This is why you see them so often at major transitions in life. Births, deaths, marriages – all the major ceremonies which mark these important times in our lives – have rituals associated with them. And these rituals are attempts to control events which aren't necessarily controllable.

NW: *You also see these rituals when people gamble.*

BH: That's right. It's well established that gamblers are very superstitious, as are many sports people. This is the irony: it turns out that these superstitious rituals are quite beneficial because if you stop a sportsperson performing a ritual then they often don't perform as well. So this habitual way of behaving can actually be beneficial.

NW: *Is there any practical impact of the research you've been doing on the supernatural?*

BH: It's important to recognise that a lot of practices are potentially very dangerous. In Africa there's a widespread belief that if you have sex with a virgin you can cure AIDS. I think that's a manifestation of essentialism about youth and the power of youth. People believe that by being intimate with the young they can somehow absorb their vitality. In literature you'll find many examples of this style of thinking. Dracula provides another example of this notion of absorbing the essence of individuals. In cultures where magical thinking is very prevalent, though, people are certainly suffering.

NW: *I'm interested in the case of original works of art. Many people feel that the original work by the great artist is the one that carries all the value, presumably because it has somehow been in touch with the artist. But when you discover that what you took to be an original is an excellent copy or pastiche, you may lose interest in the image. Is that magical thinking, or is there something else going on in these cases?*

BH: No, it's not purely magical thinking because there's also an issue about supply and demand. If you could reproduce everything then there would be no limit. Part of the value that we place on objects comes from the fact that if everybody wants them, and there's a limited supply, then you can ask more for them. That's just basic economics. But there's something about owning stuff that belonged to celebrities which conveys or triggers essentialist notions. This is why it's not just the owning of it; it's the touching of it, it's the coveting of it, it's the intimacy with the object which make it so important. So, for example, there was a company in Hollywood doing a roaring trade in reselling celebrity clothing: they offered a cleaning service, but nobody wanted it. I think it speaks to this idea that you literally have part of George Clooney, or whoever else you look up to, in your clothing.

One of the common criticisms I hear about this notion of essentialism is that it isn't different from pure association. If you feel repulsed by Fred West's cardigan, that is because when you think about Fred West you have all these associated negative thoughts. Why do you need to invoke a belief in some underlying energy or spiritual dimension to explain that?

One of the best counterexamples to that way of thinking is this. Imagine a hypothetical situation where you have two books that you can hold. One book has vast amounts of detail associated with Adolf Hitler. That book should trigger negative thoughts about Hitler, and that should be a book you wouldn't particularly want to hold. But I bet my bottom dollar that if the other book was a cookery book with no information about Hitler, and yet you discovered that he had often used it and held it intimately, that's the book you would find repugnant. It's the notion that there's a physical connection that triggers the negativity, that their essence can transform or contaminate the physical world. That, of course, is a completely supernatural belief: it's not an association.

NW: *Do you think all of these cases of essentialism derive from a misplaced theory of contagion?*

BH: That's exactly my hypothesis. It's because we're not sure why people may be evil or why they're repugnant that we take these precautions. We adopt this biological model of contagion, which is a very useful adaptation.

NW: *You're a psychologist and psychology is usually seen as falling within the social sciences. Do you identify yourself as a social scientist?*

BH: Psychology has an identity crisis. It's misrepresented in the media, and the general public holds preconceptions about it. But when you discover more about the different areas of research that go on, you soon discover that it has applications beyond the social sciences. Much of what I'm interested in connects with brain science or neuroscience. I'm also interested in artificial intelligence. The notion of the mind goes beyond simple social sciences. I'm greatly reassured by Darwin, because if you look at his *On the Origin of Species*, in the last few pages he talks about how if you really want to understand mankind it's not enough simply to understand evolution in a physical sense: you have to understand the evolution of the mind. I find that gratifying, especially when some of my colleagues from the 'harder' sciences, such as physics and chemistry, label psychology a non-science.

FURTHER READING

Steven Pinker, *How the Mind Works* (Penguin, 1997)
Paul Bloom, *Descartes' Baby: How Child Development Explains What Makes Us Human* (Basic Books, 2004)
Nicholas Humphrey, *Soul Dust: The Magic of Consciousness* (Quercus, 2012)

15

DOREEN MASSEY ON SPACE

Doreen Massey is Emeritus Professor of Geography at the Open University. Her books include *Spatial Divisions of Labour*, *Space, Place and Gender*, *For Space*, and *World City*. She focuses on space, place, regional inequality, globalisation, and cities. Most recently, she is co-author and editor, with Stuart Hall and Michael Rustin, of *The Kilburn Manifesto* [http://lwbooks.co.uk/journals/soundings/manifesto.html], published in book form by Lawrence and Wishart, 2015.

David Edmonds: *Doreen Massey has made her reputation by studying space. Not outer space – space here on planet Earth. Professor Massey is a geographer who wants us to rethink many of our assumptions about space, including the assumption that it is simply something we pass through. She believes that an analysis of spatial relations – between, for example, people, cities, jobs – is key to an understanding of politics and power.*

Nigel Warburton: *The topic we're focusing on is space. Some people might think that that's a topic for physicists or architects; why is it a topic for geographers?*

Doreen Massey: If history is about time, geography is about space. What I do in geography is not space meaning 'outer space', or space meaning 'atomic space'. It is space as that dimension of the world in which we live. Whereas historians concentrate on the temporal dimension, how things change over time, what geographers concentrate on is the way in which things are arranged – we would often say 'geographically'; I say, 'over space'.

NW: *And in your own work about space what do you focus on?*

DM: One of the things that motivated me was anger. I got really annoyed with the rest of the social sciences, and indeed with philosophers, paying so much attention to time, so that space became a residual dimension: it's always 'time', and 'space'. Time is the dimension of change, of dynamism, of the life we live, and all the rest of it. Space became the dimension that wasn't all of that. A lot of us, implicitly, think of space as a kind of flat surface out there – we 'cross space'. And space is therefore devoid of temporality: it is without time, it is without dynamism, it is a flat, inert given. Foucault wrote in the later part of his life that we often think of space like that, and that was wrong. And I agree with Foucault about this.

A lot of what I've been trying to do over my all-too-many years when writing about space is to bring space alive, to dynamise it, and to make it relevant, to emphasise how important space is in the lives in which we live, and in the organisation of the societies in which we live. Most obviously I would say that space is not a flat surface across which we walk. Raymond Williams discussed this. When you're taking a train across the landscape, you're not travelling across a dead, flat, surface that is space. You're cutting across a myriad of ongoing stories. Instead of space being a flat surface, it's more like a pincushion of a million stories. If you stop at any point in that journey, there will be a story. Raymond Williams spoke about looking out of a train window and there was this woman clearing the grate. He speeds on and forever in his mind she's stuck in that moment. But actually, of course, that woman is in the middle of doing something; it's a story. Maybe she's going away tomorrow to see her sister, but before she goes she really must clean that grate out because she's been meaning to do it for ages. So I want to see space as a cut through the myriad stories in which we are all living at any one moment. Space and time become intimately connected.

NW: *If space isn't just an empty stage, if it's somehow inhabited and imbued with all kinds of stories and memories and events, how can you study it?*

DM: There are a million ways to answer that! But one way is to say that it raises some of the most acute questions. If time is the dimension in which things happen one after the other, the dimension of succession, then space is the dimension of things existing at the same time: of simultaneity. It's the dimension of multiplicity. We're sitting here, and it's around midday in London. Well, at this moment it is already night in the Far East; my friends in Latin America are just stirring and thinking about getting up. Space is the dimension that cuts across all those stories; the dimension of our simultaneity, of multiplicity. What that means is that space is the dimension that presents us with the existence of 'the other'. It presents me with the existence of those friends in Latin America. It is space that presents us with the question of the social. And it presents us with the most fundamental of political questions, which is, how are we going to live together?

NW: *So you're saying that space isn't about physical locality so much as relations between human beings?*

DM: Exactly. We don't think of time as being material. Time is thought of as ethereal, virtual, without materiality. Whereas space is thought of as material: it is the land out there. But there's a dimension of space that is equally abstract – just a dimension. That's the way in which I want to think about it. Space concerns our relations with each other and in fact social space, I would say, is a product of our relations with each other, our connections with each other. Globalisation, for instance, is a new geography constructed out of the relations we have with each other across the globe. And the most important issue that that raises, if we are really thinking socially, is that all those relations are going to be filled with power. So what we have is a geography which is the geography of power. The distribution of those relations mirrors the power relations within our society.

NW: *Could you give an example?*

DM: Look at the city in which we're sitting, London. The power relations that run from the City Square Mile and from Canary Wharf around the rest of the world are extraordinary. London is a key node within the financial globalisation that has taken place over the last 30 years – part of the dominance of finance within the organisation of the global economy. Some of the most powerful institutions are here, and it was also here that a lot of the neo-liberal economics, within which we now live, was imagined in the first place. And London has been part of the export of that way of thinking around the world. So its power is more than economic, it's also political and ideological.

NW: *You've given a description of power relations in the City, but how is that **political**?*

DM: There are a number of ways in which that way of looking at globalisation can lead you into asking political questions — which is what I want to do. It enables you to map power relations. I'm not against power — power is the ability to do things. What I think we should be critical of in the social sciences is the unequal distribution of power: the power of some groups over others, the power of some places over others. I am very critical of the role of the City of London in its domination of economies and economic ideologies in the rest of the world. So, one way into this topic is through an empirical, descriptive examination which identifies that the power in our globalised world is too unequally distributed. But there's another way. This relates back to how we think about space. The way in which we look at globalisation at the moment turns space into time. For instance, in our terminology we are a 'developed' country; the countries 'behind us' are 'developing'; and then you've also got 'underdeveloped' countries. Now what that does is to convert contemporaneous differences between countries into a single linear history. It's saying that that country over there — let's say Argentina, a 'developing' country — isn't a country at the same moment, which is different. Rather, it's a country which is following our historical path to become a 'developed' country like ours. So we are denying the simultaneity, the multiplicity of space, that I want to insist on, and turning all those differences into a single historical trajectory.

Now that has a lot of political repercussions. The most important one is that it assumes that there is only one future, and that's being a 'developed' country. Argentina must follow the way we are going. Well, as it happens, Argentina right now does not want to follow the way we are going. There are a lot of alternative voices in Latin America that are saying 'We don't want to be "developed" like you. We want a different model, which is more egalitarian, more communitarian, and so forth.' But that way of turning space into time, turning geography into history, is a way of denying the possibility of doing something different. If we take space seriously as the dimension of multiplicity then it opens up politics to the possibility of alternatives.

NW: *So you're trying to encourage a* Gestalt *shift by describing the world in a particular way, to reveal a different way of understanding the same phenomena?*

DM: Absolutely. If we took space seriously as a dimension that we create through our power relations, and as a dimension which presents us with the multiplicity of the world, and refused to align all stories into one story of development, then we would reimagine the world in a different way. We are presented with different political questions. I think it opens up our minds!

NW: *You've criticised the categorisation of 'developing' countries and 'underdeveloped' countries and the implication that there is only one trajectory towards the system that we have in the west. What can you do to persuade those who believe in that trajectory? How can you convince somebody in the grip of that ideology that they're wrong?*

DM: People get trapped in their imaginations: that's a common problem. So it's a question of challenging common sense. The hegemonic common sense at the moment includes the notion that we are stuck with this. And I hope that my arguments about space will help us break out of this feeling that we can't do anything about it. I do little things: I talk all over the place, I write, I go to and work in countries that are trying to do something different.

NW: *Is the problem that each society wants to project its version of reality onto the rest of the world?*

DM: Well, I don't want to attribute nefarious intentions to people. I would say two things. One is that that way of thinking – 'one road' if you like – is characteristic of modernism and modernity generally, on both left and right of the political spectrum.

There is one thing called 'development', there is one thing called 'progress': it's what's been called 'grand narratives'. This was a feature of some versions of Marxism too: from feudalism we would go to capitalism, to socialism, and then to communism. But this idea of a grand narrative is also highly political and very much a product of power relations. There is no doubt that the leaders of the Western world and the banks in the City want the rest of the world to follow and to be dominated by their model of the world. The USA and the UK are involved in trying to force other countries into what they call democracy, which usually means market societies. So there's both an overall *Zeitgeist*, the grand narrative, which is a hundred years old and which we have criticised a lot in the social sciences. And there is a particular political dimension in which the powerful want to dragoon the rest into following their path.

NW: *Are there other ways in which space and politics link together?*

DM: There are loads of ways. For instance, do you remember Occupy London, that group of tents? I got a little bit involved in that. I gave a couple of lectures in the university tent. What struck me was how spatial their politics were. For one thing there was a huddle – a very unpretentious low huddle of tents between vast stone edifices of God and Mammon on each side. The very unpretentiousness of those tents was an affront to the pretentiousness of St Paul's and the London Stock Exchange. The very physicality of those tents raised an impertinent finger to the complacent spaces of the Establishment and neo-liberalism. There was something really symbolic about the very placing of the thing itself and its material form. And even though it was so tiny, I think that's the reason it had to go. In its very presence it was posing questions that were too deep to ask.

NW: *'Occupy' even by its name was about space. The movement occupied space.*

DM: That's right. What they did was to create a new kind of space. One of the things that neo-liberalism – if one can use that awful word – has done to our cities is to privatise a lot of what was once public space. That's one thing those in the Occupy movement, and others too, have complained about.

They tried to set up the camp outside the Stock Exchange. They were told they couldn't because that square is private space – although you would not know from looking at it. The place where they eventually set up their camps was public space in the sense that it wasn't private. People passed through every day, and so on. But that's public space in a very loose sense of the word 'public'. What fascinated me about Occupy was that they were able to create public space in a more meaningful sense. They created a space in which people didn't just pass by each other on the way to work or the shops. They talked, they conversed, they argued. While I was there people who had nothing to do with the occupation came up to me and talked and asked questions. It seemed to me that what Occupy managed briefly to create was a real public space, a place for the creation of a public, of politically engaged subjects, of people who would talk to each other about the wider world. We need a lot more of this kind of space, a space that brings us together to talk and to argue about the kind of future world we want.

NW: *Do you think geography as a subject can be a catalyst for this kind of development?*

DM: I think it can. A greater appreciation of geography and why it matters, and why in the end space is utterly political, is very important. Look at this country at the moment: there's a huge divide between the north and south. OK, everybody knows that. I argue that that matters, it changes the society in which we live: there are different cultures between north and south, different politics. What's more, it makes the inequality between different people in this country even worse. People who own properties in the south are making money hand over fist, just through the rise in property prices, far more than they are making from their jobs. My friends in Liverpool and Manchester aren't making that money. So the very division between north and south is increasing the inequality between us. Geography matters. Or again, think about gender. The history of the division between private spaces and public places has been crucial in the history of gender difference between men and women, and the confinement for centuries of women to private space, while men are the public figures in the public space.

NW:　*Geography is usually thought of as one of the social sciences: do you think of yourself as a social scientist?*

DM:　I do. In fact a lot of my life has been spent trying to urge the social sciences to take geography more seriously. Geography is a very multi-disciplinary discipline. We engage a lot with sociologists and economists. But one of the things that I like most about geography is that it also includes people who are natural scientists: people who study rivers and mountain formation and the Antarctic. I think within geography there is the possibility of bringing together the social and the natural sciences more than we have historically done. There are vast differences between them, and the process is very hard, but we need to do this. In an age in which we face environmental problems, climate change, pollution, problems which are utterly social too, I think that the natural and the social sciences need to talk to each other more. And geography is one of the places that this could happen – and one of the reasons that I love the discipline.

FURTHER READING

Doreen Massey, *Space, Place and Gender* (Polity Press, 1994)
Doreen Massey, *For Space* (Sage, 2005)
David Featherstone, *Resistance, Space and Political Identities* (Wiley-Blackwell, 2008)

SECTION 4

POLITICS &
SOCIAL SCIENCE

16

CRAiG CALHOUN ON PROTEST MOVEMENTS

 Craig Calhoun has been Director and President of the London School of Economics and Political Science since 2012. He is an advocate for interdisciplinary education, research and public engagement, and is known for studies of critical social theory, nationalism, democratic politics, social movements, technological change, and the future of capitalism.

David Edmonds: *Protest movements take many shapes and forms, from feminism, to the demonstrations in Tiananmen Square, to today's 'Occupy'. But how are protest movements formed and organised? How and why do they succeed or fail? What, if anything, do they have in common? The sociologist and Director of the London School of Economics, Craig Calhoun, has made the study of protest movements a lifelong project.*

Nigel Warburton: *The topic we are going to focus on is protest movements, and this is a topic that you have done quite a lot of empirical research on. Could you begin by saying something about that?*

Craig Calhoun: I've worked on movements in a variety of different settings, from the 19th century in Britain, France and the US, to the more recent Tiananmen Square protests in China in 1989, and on to thinking about Occupy Wall Street and more recent protest in the US and Europe.

Protests are a tactic: people use protests as one of the tools to try to get media attention, to try to get issues put on the public agenda, to try to get policy-makers to address those issues. But it's only one tactic, so the same groups may also be engaged in other kinds of activities at the same time. A movement is the longer process of change; when we talk about, say, the feminist movement, there were protests, but they weren't the whole thing.

NW: *I'm really interested in how a social scientist approaches an event like the protests in Tiananmen Square in 1989. There were journalists there; there were historians who have written about these events in relation to China. What does a social scientist have to contribute here?*

CC: I'd like to tell you that because I was a social scientist I somehow knew these protests were coming and I planned a research project around it. In fact I was teaching in Beijing that year, and so my students were part of the protest movement, and I was able to observe some of the early developments that helped pave the way for it.

Social scientists are interested in movements and protests because they have an important role in bringing social change. But protests also require social organisation that depends on pre-existing social relationships. So to give you an example from China, one of the things that you notice is that there are large crowds, big marches, big gatherings in Tiananmen Square. Well, how is that organised, who comes out, how do they get out? People marched, often in groups that corresponded to their courses of study and their classes in the university. The ties, the links that they had to each other from their dormitories, from their classes, were used to organise the protest. Then when they put up tents and camped out in Tiananmen Square, they were also using pre-existing organisational ties, but they were trying to give a symbolic message that they were capable of organising, that 'the people' could be orderly, could be organised; and therefore the government claim, that without the government there would be no order, was shown to be false. So on both the input side, how things get organised, and the output side, what message gets sent, there is a strong social science element.

NW: *That case was particularly interesting because the message sent from Tiananmen Square as received in the West was about democracy, but to some people there, as I understand it, it was about corruption.*

CC: Well the two are not unrelated, but the slogans that were used were often different in English and Chinese, and people picked up on different things. As you can imagine, reporters who spoke only English received the messages the students put in English. Because this was a protest of students, and to some extent intellectuals, they were often people who spoke English and could craft the message, and they knew that a message about democracy would have a wide appeal. That didn't mean that they were not sincere about democracy, only that they knew that message would catch the reporters. They knew that a message about corruption would catch members of the Chinese working class. It's just like a Western politician who has different messages when he's speaking to a trade union group, when he's speaking to a group of university students, when he's speaking to parliament. Messages are crafted for occasions.

The story of the protest had several roots. One of them was corruption: the terrible inefficiency and even theft, the taking of money and using it for bad ends. Another was the extent to which the system failed to deliver economic development and a strong country: that corruption undermined the government. So you had a government that was in one sense strong, and people might object to some of the uses of power, but corruption meant it wasn't able to do the things people wanted a government to do. There was the message 'We need China to be a stronger country. The government needs to be less corrupt, more efficient'. That connected to students in particular because, as young intellectuals, they were thinking what you need are well-trained people who have the expertise that we have. The message about the government was partly that if you aren't creating opportunities for well-educated people to assume leadership roles, you'll make the country weaker. That then connected to a national self-strengthening message: we want China to be strong. They knew that that wasn't the message that foreigners wanted to hear, but it also then connected to democracy, that the people wanted something better of the government.

NW: *Now, I can see how that sort of social analysis sheds new light on events that have perhaps been caricatured in some of the media, but is it purely descriptive? Are you simply analysing what's happened? Do you want things to change? Is there, built into your social science, a critique of what was going on?*

CC: Social science opens up at least three different registers of engagement here. One of them is description. Description is really important because we want to know, in thorough and balanced ways, what goes on, and what went on historically. So, part of the description includes the fact that this wasn't the first time there were large-scale protests in Tiananmen Square. Past events shape the present.

Then there's a causal analysis; why did this happen? Why did it happen *when* it happened? What were the necessary conditions we might not have known about that were part of making this protest happen? In fact there were people organising and getting ready for this protest months before anything happened in public, so tracing the causal chain of events that made it possible becomes important.

But the third register of engagement involves normative questions: having a critical understanding. That doesn't just mean saying 'I object to it and I criticise it'; it may mean asking 'Well, why did they do it this way? What were the other possibilities? Would it have gone better if they had tried a different tactic?' Social science can open up a variety of avenues for critical analysis of movements, as other social phenomena, and anyone reading that social science can then bring their own different values to it. You come with the value that, say, 'I would like there to be more widespread egalitarian popular participation because I believe in democracy.' Then you might have a criticism of the elitism of the students as intellectuals who tended to want to keep this a very intellectually-focused protest, and not reach out as much to workers. That's a question partly of the values, but partly of knowing descriptively how much they reached out to the workers, knowing whether they had connections and channels, whether that was even possible, knowing the reasons why they didn't. So all of those are part of social science.

NW: *How did you go about researching what was going on in Tiananmen Square? It's not obvious where you could start.*

CC: It's a great question, and in this particular case it gives me the chance to illustrate different social science methods, because my research was based on multiple methods. That's not always the case. But there I was, living in China, indeed in university-owned housing there, with students, and so I was able, in first-hand observation, to see this growing, to talk with people before some of the protests, to follow the marches into Tiananmen Square from the Haidian District, to spend time with the people during the occupation, and so forth. So first-hand participant observation – walking alongside them during the march – is the first way in which I was gathering information.

The second part of this was with a group of students I developed a questionnaire, and we conducted a sample survey of the occupation of students who were engaged in the occupation of Tiananmen Square to try to find out what it meant to them, and to try to find out what differences there were. For example, did people from Beijing, or from the provinces, look at this differently or those from different universities or working in different fields? Did scientists look at this differently from humanists, or social scientists (and indeed they did)? So one method we used was surveys. I then followed up by doing retrospective interviews. Over the next couple of years, I went and interviewed leaders of the protest, and then others who'd been involved in the protest in a different way, using oral history techniques to find out what they could tell me about this.

Finally, I used documentary research, which is more common to historians, to find out what had been printed in different leaflets; what the government police reports, to the extent they were available, had said; what the media had reported about the events; and so forth. I even used film: I went to CNN's archive of footage they had acquired to look at many different films. I'll give you a quick example of why it matters. As a participant observer you get first-hand knowledge, which we often value a great deal. But you have a kind of worm's-eye view, not a bird's-eye view: you're right in the middle, so if you're in the middle of literally a million people in Tiananmen Square, you hear and see what is going on right around you, but you don't get a picture of the whole thing. Using film as a source, you can see it from different angles: here's what it looked like from the Beijing Hotel; here's what it looked like from the Monument to the People's Heroes; and so you can get a bigger overview of what's going on. Even in estimating crowd size, I did things like figure out how many people stood on one of the paving stones. There are paving stones several feet square that pave Tiananmen Square; about eight or nine people stand on one of those. And then later

I worked out how many paving stones there are, how much open space, and how much was filled with the Monument to the People's Heroes or other things; so to be able to say the crowd was a quarter of a million, or a million and a half, was something that took a bit of work.

NW: *Calling yourself a social scientist involves the 'social' part, but the 'science' aspect is sometimes less obvious to some outsiders. In a case like this, is there a scientific way of analysing all those different sorts of sources of information, the data as it were, that come to you? Or is it a matter of an individual making a subjective assessment about what's important and what isn't?*

CC: I would reject that forced choice, but it points to a key question. People mean many different things by 'science', so we could start by saying 'Are you really systematic in gathering the data, rather than only gathering the data that proves your preconception?' Just being systematic is the beginning of science. Then there are the different methodologies used to try to gather the data, but also to test your preliminary conclusions. You can also go on to specific methods: in the natural or 'hard' sciences, we often use experiments; we often use mathematical models. And there are certain techniques that people think of as particularly scientific that add rigour and precision to research. Some of these don't fit as well into the kind of study I was doing in Tiananmen Square: there wasn't an easy experimental model. You use the methods that fit with the problem you're studying and the setting in which you're studying it, but trying to use whatever methods can yield systematic reliable data and then trying to cross-check to find out whether the first impressions you get are correct – I think is a very basic definition of science.

NW: *The social sciences have been attacked recently for not delivering in various ways, or for delivering political messages that aren't palatable to those who are funding the social sciences. How can you keep the rigour of your discipline yet not kowtow to those who are funding you?*

CC: There have been some highly publicised attacks such as the US Congress on the National Science Foundation for funding political science research. Some of the attacks were themselves, of course, politically motivated: political scientists tell us things we don't want to hear, therefore we should stop funding the research. There's an anxiety on the part of some conservatives in government that political and social scientists are too liberal; but at other times the opposite is also true: there are protestors saying social scientists are too conservative.

Social science has a problem with this because it studies things that are very topical – not everything. Some things social scientists study don't make headlines; they aren't interesting to the press. But lots of things social scientists do matter to policy-makers, so policy-makers have opinions about them. Many of them are being argued about in public. Social science has the potential to shape the argument. I like to think that social science often raises the quality of both sides of the argument; that if we have better knowledge about an issue, you can make better left-wing or better right-wing arguments about the issue. But because these things are so much argued over, then the social scientific research itself becomes controversial. Of course natural science is not immune to this – think of the fight over evolution, which became just as controversial an issue as that social scientists study.

We also should recognise that social science does necessarily involve interpretation that cannot be reduced to perfectly objective results. Even when you have something that seems to be objective – you have a photograph of Tiananmen Square, for example – there are still questions: What knowledge do you bring to that to interpret it? Do you say 'Well there's some building over there on the left', or do you say 'That building is Mao's tomb.' The way in which people behave is shaped by it being Mao's tomb. These various layers of interpretation mean that the kind of knowledge that is generated depends on the care that goes into the interpretation. You can never completely escape that; even if you use a survey or you do an experiment, it doesn't completely escape this interpretation.

Some people set up a standard; they say 'If it can't completely escape the element of interpretation, it won't count as science.' That same argument would actually kill science.

NW: *In interviewing a range of social scientists I've been struck by the fact that sociologists tend to identify themselves strongly as social* *scientists; whereas economists and psychologists see themselves as primarily economists or psychologists. Do you think there really is some natural kind, 'the social sciences', or is it just an artificial category that's been created by universities?*

CC: Wonderful observation. I think that there is no natural kind. We have historically shaped a division of labour for looking at the world. There was a time, 35 years ago, when the observation you made would not have been equally true, when economists and psychologists would have been more likely to call themselves social scientists. There was a time when the sociologists were part of the American Economics Association. Since then, psychology and economics have been two of the fastest-growing social sciences. During the last third of a century, they've been very successful and they've changed. Economics has become more autonomous and much more mathematical and more oriented to micro-foundations rather than macro-work, and more driven by a way of abstracting from reality in order to theorise, and become more separate in many ways from the other social sciences. This is now changing a little bit: economists are now moving back into looking at a variety of other social issues. Psychology became more and more tied to the natural sciences, to neuroscience, to psychopharmacology, to biological research, and so psychology also moved. These had material elements, so you can do a sociological analysis of it. You can point out that the rise of business schools shaped what happened with economics; that psychology departments often moved from the social science division in universities, to the natural science division in universities; that the number of psychologists doing field research or surveys went down; and the number of psychologists focusing on experiments, and especially experiments that involved apparatus physically engaging the brain and so forth, went up.

So, the change wasn't just a change of attitudes and professional pride: it was a change in the actual organisation of the work of the different fields. Anthropology, sociology, political science and so forth remained more clearly parts of social science, although some people in each of them might say 'We should emulate the economists and psychologists; maybe we should use neuroscience too, or maybe we should develop mathematical models based on individual choice', and there are a lot of political scientists, and some sociologists, who do that.

There's no natural order to this, this is a human social process of creating organisation, just like creating nation-states:
there's no natural line between most countries. Where there
is a line on a map, it has come to be developed historically and
it's backed up by state power, and there are sometimes trea-
ties. It's the same with academic disciplines: there's a sociological process that includes things like the formation of
disciplinary departments, and so if you didn't decide to organise universities in departments, you wouldn't get the same
disciplines. The founders of many of these fields are the same.
We could look at Adam Smith, and see a great founder of
economics, but he was also a great founder of sociology, and
the book he considered his most important was *The Theory of
Moral Sentiments*: he was a great philosopher; he was in fact a
professor of moral philosophy. So this kind of history is one
where there was one way of organising intellectual life that
gives way to others over time.

NW: *To take the next step from that description, are you happy with the
division that you've inherited of the social sciences? Are you saying
that they should change and open up into more fluid ways of
describing activities and research projects?*

CC: I would prefer the social sciences to have more fluid connections
across various boundaries: methodologically, but also in disciplinary and other terms. A great social scientist, the sociologist Immanuel Wallerstein, called for a project of 'opening the
social sciences', in which, among other things, he imagined a
reconfiguration by method. He asked 'What if all the people
who do participant observation field work, whether they are
anthropologists or sociologists, or whatever, go together, and
all the people who do comparative historical work producing
big picture histories go together, and all the people who do
quantitative research go together?' That would be a different
mixture, and some of that happens. Doing it all by method
would be a mistake: what we need is the fluidity to be able to
sometimes divide up by method in order to improve our
methods and deepen the work in that method, and sometimes bring people with different methods together because
they're interested in the same problem.

Say you're interested in urbanisation – a huge issue in the world,
obviously a major sociological question. The majority of the

world's people now live in cities: cities are growing extremely rapidly; some are bringing massive economic gains, but there are also slums. Financing urban infrastructure is probably the biggest financial challenge in the world, but it's also an anthropological or cultural question: what is happening to local cultures, to neighbourhoods? Are people developing new cultures? This can be a matter of creativity in the arts, but also a matter of violent conflicts: almost small-scale civil wars in some cases, new sorts of security challenges. You can see the phenomenon of urbanisation in several different ways, and it's important that we do that.

What I suggest would be desirable is more willingness within the social sciences to create mixtures. I think we should study topics and problems that are important in the world like inequality or urbanisation. Topics yield one kind of grouping, and this brings people together from different disciplines. But at the same time, improving methods is also important and people who use the same research techniques should work together to improve them. And social scientists can form groups by theoretical perspectives like rational choice theory or Marxism or cultural analysis. Disciplines can be important too, creating connections among people who work on different problems and use different methods and theories but who share analytic perspectives and ideas about how things connect up. Disciplines are also useful for quality control. The mistake, I think, is letting one of these completely dominate over the others. Today, the biggest risk is that disciplines will be the enemies of flexibility and therefore inhibit creativity and innovation and indeed practical contributions.

FURTHER READING

Craig Calhoun, *Neither Gods Nor Emperors: Students and the Struggle for Democracy in China* (University of California Press, 1994)

Craig Calhoun, *The Roots of Radicalism* (University of Chicago Press, 2012)

James M. Jasper, *The Art of Moral Protest: Culture, Biography, and Creativity in Social Movements* (University of Chicago, 1997)

Doug McAdam, Sidney Tarrow, and Charles Tilly, *The Dynamics of Contention* (Cambridge University Press, 2001)

Alain Touraine, *The Voice and the Eye* (Cambridge University Press, 1981)

17

DANNY DORLING ON INEQUALITY

Danny Dorling joined the School of Geography and the Environment at the University of Oxford in September 2013 to take up the Halford Mackinder Professorship in Geography. He was previously a Professor of Geography at the University of Sheffield. He has also worked in Newcastle, Bristol, Leeds, and New Zealand. He went to university in Newcastle upon Tyne, and to school in Oxford.

David Edmonds: *When in 2004 steel tycoon Lakshmi Mittal paid a cool £57million for a property in London's Kensington Palace Gardens, it was – at the time – the most expensive home in Britain. Mittal has since bought additional properties for much more; and in any case, the price looks a bargain compared to his yacht. The gap between rich and poor has grown dramatically over the past few decades: not just in terms of wealth, but on other indicators too – there's been a growing gap in life expectancy, for example. Danny Dorling is a social scientist, a human geographer. He's analysed trends in inequality and presented the data in novel and compelling ways. He claims inequality is bad for everyone: not just for the poor, but even, bizarrely, for Mr Mittal and the rest of the super-rich.*

Nigel Warburton: *The topic we're focusing on is inequality. Could you give us a quick sketch of the degree of current inequality in the rich world.*

Danny Dorling: Currently inequality in the rich world is at a high: it's been rising for several decades and if you measure it in terms of differences in life expectancy, or in terms of income and wealth differences, it's the highest it's been since around the 1920s, maybe even earlier.

NW: *So the disparity between rich and poor is massive and higher than it's been for years?*

DD: Yes. Of course most people are much better off than they were 80 or 90 years ago. But the gaps between groups of people have become as wide again as they were back then, and that is staggering; it's one of the defining features of our times.

NW: *Why do you think it's happened?*

DD: To put it very crudely, a lot of us took our eyes off the ball and didn't fight enough to keep it down. There were some groups who thought inequality wasn't necessarily a bad thing in a time of riches because, the argument went, a few people getting richer would help drag everybody else up. But there are wider forces that make society more unequal unless you do something about it.

NW: *What sort of forces are you talking about?*

DD: If you leave a group of people alone there will tend to be variation between them, which grows enormously if not controlled. Some people will like making money much more than others, and if you let them do it, they'll make yet more money: they're driven by money. If you don't curtail their wish to make money, they'll become richer and richer and you then get imbalances of power. If you simply leave particular social situations to run their course, you tend to get growing inequalities in income, and then even bigger inequalities in wealth. Then, with a lag, you see rising inequalities of people's wider life chances in some of the most important things such as education and health.

NW: *So you've touched on it there, but why should we care that there are these inequalities? If people reach a threshold level of income, why would it matter if there are some very rich people?*

DD: Well, you can carry on for quite a long time with high and growing inequality and it might not appear to matter terribly much, particularly if the economy as a whole is growing. If the entire country is becoming richer, and rich people are becoming much, much richer, but poor people are still getting a little bit more than the generation before them, it's possible to keep things going. There are great ecological and sustainability problems with this approach: your overall consumption levels are enormous. But one reason that inequalities have become so high again is that it's not that uncomfortable becoming more unequal if you're all becoming a bit richer. What's really uncomfortable is when you have economic decline coupled with high and rising inequalities; and what's almost impossible to live with is when you have economic decline, most people getting poorer, the poor getting very poor, and a few people still getting richer.

NW: *And it's uncomfortable because people are just envious of the rich?*

DD: The argument about envy fits with the scenario in which economies are growing and everybody is becoming a bit better off while the rich are gaining even more than the poor. What happens when you have economic decline is the switch from envy to disgust. It's not just people saying during austerity 'I wish I could be the one rich person.' Instead, people say 'In a time of austerity, what are they doing taking 50% pay rises?'

NW: *Well, one common argument is that the people who get those huge pay rises earn them. There's something they do, by their own merit, which justifies the pay differential.*

DD: This is an argument that you could try to sell when you have economic growth. The very rich could say you're all having growth because of us. But it is an argument which becomes unsustainable, when entire countries are becoming poorer, for the very rich to say 'We're doing something that's so valuable that you need to give us a 50% pay rise this year.' You really have to believe that without them everything would fall apart.

NW: *Well, take sport: there are people who can run a marathon in around two hours, and that's quite phenomenal. There are huge individual differences in sporting skill and aptitude. What makes you so sure that there aren't huge individual differences in terms of people's capacity to generate income, and to do things which are worthwhile for society?*

DD: I don't think that differences in ability to run between human beings are that great. Human beings are remarkably similar animals. If you look at leg length and height and what we are capable of, we're not talking about different species that can do different things. The extent to which people can walk and run very much depends on the environment in which they are brought up to walk and run in. And of course you can always take an individual and train them up to behave in a particular way. You can do the same with a dog. That doesn't mean that any one dog's a particularly special dog: it means somebody's trained that dog to behave in that particular way. What's remarkable about human beings is how similar we are. We almost all have binocular vision; we almost all have two opposable thumbs; we all have a brain of a particular size (it doesn't vary that much – in fact you don't want a really big one because that's actually associated with a form of mental illness). But we're very bad at recognising how similar we are; and for peculiar reasons we're very good at looking at the slight differences and then trying to make out that they're terribly important.

NW: *You seem to be saying that inequality is bad. Is it bad because it leads to certain other ills, or is it intrinsically bad?*

DD: There are always differences between people and there are always variations, but where inequalities are not based on something which is real, they can have very sad implications. One of my favourite examples is singing. There's a lovely history of human beings singing; people have written about Neanderthals singing! And if you look at the distribution of singing (how many people are used to singing), it's very high in parts of Africa, and it's now pretty low in parts of Europe. But we have this idea that only a few people can be great singers – you have to win The X-Factor and then you get to make records. And what ends up happening is that most people stop singing and you put a few people on pedestals and say what wonderful singers they are. It's not just singing, it's storytelling; it's all kinds of human abilities. You get a 'winner takes all' society, where most people feel that their achievements aren't good enough and a few people are told that they're so good that they begin to believe they're super-human.

NW: *In the singing example you're saying that potentially almost anybody has the ability to sing at a quite good level, and only social* *factors stop them from doing that. Now, are you saying that economic inequality is one of the obstacles to various kinds of achievement, or rather that quite apart from its consequences, gross economic inequality is just wrong – it's a bad thing?*

DD: It's quite hard to tell whether economic inequality is just a bad thing in and of itself, or whether it's inefficient. There are so many overlapping reasons why high levels of inequality cause harm in all kinds of ways, that it's very hard to disentangle. It's a bit like saying 'Is there a good way of smoking tobacco?' The key thing about tobacco is – although I happen to quite like tobacco – it's bad for you. Tobacco is just not good, and inequality is simply not good. I'm not saying we should all be completely equal or never smoke, but great levels of inequality tend to bring harm in all kinds of ways. They harm our creativity, they harm our economy, they harm our health. And they mean that we delude ourselves at the top of society as well as at the bottom.

NW: *And yet, if you take the example of Renaissance Florence, it was great social inequality that allowed the wonderful artists that were commissioned by the Medici or whoever to flourish.*

DD: No. No. No. No. No! It was the Medicis accepting the illegitimate son of a peasant woman, Leonardo da Vinci, and allowing him to sit not just at the end of the table but next to the lord. It was the equality of the Medici times, at least around their table, that led to that. They had an attitude which was unusual, and was breaking against the old hierarchies of inequality. The sons and daughters of millionaires and billionaires don't become our only great artists. Art and creativity are in everybody. What happens to particularly draw it out of individuals at particular times varies. But if you look at indicators such as where are the highest proportions of scientific papers written per person, it's Finland and Sweden. If you look at where the most patents per person are, that's Japan. We have a myth, in very unequal countries like the United States and the UK, that we're particularly entrepreneurial.

NW: *So are you saying that there are no benefits from economic inequality?*

DD: I find it hard to find them. There are disbenefits from ridiculous levels of imposed equality. But I think it's hard to find an example of a place in the rich world which has become too equal for things to work.

NW: *Obviously uniformity in wealth is not a sustainable position because people would start to spend the money in the way they want to spend it; some will gamble and some won't; some will want to save, others won't. But is there anything we can do, generally, to reduce the massive levels of inequality that we now find ourselves with?*

DD: Well, the massive levels of inequality and wealth are currently reducing, at least for most people. Even in the UK, for 99% of the population, income inequality levels are lower than they were before the crash of 2008. It has only been the best-off 1% who have seen their incomes rise. Wealth inequalities rise more stubbornly. The general economic crisis of the rich countries at the moment means a reduction in international inequalities in wealth. If you want a slightly more equal world, part of what's going on is not necessarily bad. So in answer to your question 'Can you reduce inequality?', it's actually happening. Whether it carries on and is sustainable is unclear. The soft-landing for humanity is that the richest countries of the world become that little bit less rich but more equal, which is how you can tolerate being less rich, whilst poorer countries become better off, but don't have a super-elite who become very rich. This is the (ideal) point where people have enough, but you have very few who have too little, and even fewer who have too much. Social scientists concentrate on what is worse rather than what is good. For example there are reported to be more bankers in Barclays Bank in the UK earning over one million euros a year than there are people in the whole of Japan earning as much. We are right to be shocked by Barclays but we should also celebrate the relatively high equality of Japan and look for what it is about Japanese society which makes much lower salary inequality possible.

NW: *But you're talking about the vagaries of the market, and historically the way that people try to reduce massive economic inequality is through political change, including the imposition of rules to prevent the rich from getting massively richer.*

DD: Markets have always had rules. Markets are very old. We've made a mistake in the last four centuries of calling the new ways in which we live 'the market', as if there weren't markets before then. Equality makes traditional markets more equal, more efficient. The classic example is prisoners of war. When you're given your Red Cross box, prisoners swap things that they don't like: one prisoner might not like chocolate and swaps it for something that somebody else doesn't like. Markets are incredibly efficient when everybody's on the same level. Markets become really inefficient when you have a few people who have lots of money and many people who don't. People with lots of money might just buy some food because they feel like hoarding it, not because they need it. They might buy a nice-looking book, not because they want to read it but because they can and it doesn't cost very much. So inequality makes market economies inefficient.

NW: *Now, you describe yourself as a human geographer, and that's a form of social science. There is one, perhaps naïve, view of a scientist that they go out and describe the way the world is. But it seems to me you're doing much more than that.*

DD: I'm doing a little more than that. I tend to get criticised in human geography for being somebody who describes far more than almost anybody else describes, because I draw maps and pictures and look at numbers – lots of numbers, hence lots of descriptions. The way I grandly put it is this: imagine that you were a medic and you were interested in lung cancer in the early 1950s and you thought it was very complicated and there were all these possible things that could be causing lung cancer, and many theories. But you did a very simple descriptive study with doctors and smoking and you found an incredible correlation – the more that doctors seemed to smoke, the more they got lung cancer. Now, the group of social scientists who are interested in inequality in the last few years have suddenly started getting these graphs which suggest it's much more important than even they thought it was. Just like medical researchers in the 1950s, they are unsure of what is causing the correlation, but they have a series of very plausible suggestions. It's hard to remain completely neutral in that situation, but it helps to try to work out what situation you think you're in.

NW: *Well it's one thing to hypothesise about correlations and the likelihood of them being causal relations, and it seems to be another one to say 'Look this is something wrong and we ought to be changing it.' That seems a different enterprise: you're a moralist at that point.*

DD: It isn't that hard to think carefully about my philosophical position on this, because everything lines up so neatly. There isn't an affluent country in the world with high levels of inequality where other things work well. I would be a moralist, I think, if I was just against inequality, even if it had positive outcomes.

NW: *Well, if you were one of the very rich elite, there would be clear positive outcomes from large inequalities of wealth. You would be the person who gains at the expense of other people.*

DD: I might gain money. I might be able to extend my lifespan with the help of a private doctor. But I might also fear being kidnapped; I might begin to realise that people despise me; I might begin to wonder whether my partner really liked me or was just with me for the money; I might wonder what was the point of all this. I might start to distrust the servants; I might wonder if I had an honest relationship with my children or whether they lied to me (because they were relying on future inheritances and gifts). And if you look at very rich people and how some of them are giving away large amounts of their money, I think they're coming to similar conclusions about the ambiguity of great wealth.

NW: *But there are values inherent in the way you've described things. It's not as if you're giving a neutral account of economic inequality is it?*

DD: I've never seen a position where somebody has an entirely neutral view. There will be biases and values that I hold that I'm somewhat aware of. There'll be other ones that I hold that I won't be aware of at all, and it's really interesting when somebody points this out to you. But here we have a situation where everybody is losing out. The classic example is the children of the very rich, brought up by a nanny, so they don't get to see their parents and the nanny's own children who are brought up by the nanny's mother, because the nanny can't look after them. You have this chain of sadness and one of my strongest biases is that I hate chained stupidity: somebody exploiting somebody else is bad, but it's even worse when you've got everybody losing out.

NW: *When you're suggesting that greater equality would lead to better outcomes, that's a generalisation based on some kind of past evidence. Is that like a scientific law?*

DD: It's a scientific law when it comes to income and money. Money is a means to exchange. It gives you permission to do something else. So in terms of money I think you can make a claim of a scientific law. What the poor need above all else is a bit more money. When people say the poor don't need money, they haven't got the idea of poverty. And you can't all be rich: that's a scientific law. You could only all be rich if aliens came from another planet and became our slaves.

When it comes to things like improvements in education it's more complicated. For instance, I'd suggest that children on average do better in cities which are a bit more equal. The city I used to live in, Sheffield, sends more children to university than another city I used to live in, Bristol, a much more unequal city. But those are correlations. And you can try to work out what, if any, is the causal reason. Or is it just chance? And the same pattern can be found with health. You have a correlation and then you look for reasons to explain it. And one of the things about health is that a very rich person might be able to extend their life a tiny amount by paying for huge amounts of drugs, but the same amount of money can have a huge effect on thousands of babies who don't die of malaria. But you have then to prove the benefit of saving thousands of lives rather than extending one by a few years, especially if you are trying not to moralise. People tend to have fewer children when infant mortality drops. There are then fewer mouths to feed, more people grow up more healthily; more can become carers, be trained, become doctors themselves and improve overall population health. It is not that hard to show cases where the children of the rich benefited when the rich took less. Life expectancy for all social groups is now highest in those rich nations which became most equal and sustained those high levels of equality the longest.

NW: *These kinds of thoughts must be relevant to social policy and how governments implement various programmes. Do you think social science generally has something important to offer politics?*

DD: Social science always has important things to offer politics, but often there are long lags. What social science does is help to define the underlying ethos that is taught about how society operates, and that eventually influences politicians. But it may be from what they read at school. I think social scientists worry too much about trying to have an immediate policy impact, and don't take as much comfort as they should about the very long-term beneficial effects they can have if they're careful about what they do. And the greatest effects are the ones you don't notice, when the underlying belief systems of society alter.

FURTHER READING

Jamie Peck, *Constructions of Neoliberal Reason* (Oxford University Press, 2010)
Andrew Sayer, *Why We Can't Afford the Rich* (Policy Press, 2014)
Danny Dorling, *Inequality and the 1%* (Verso, 2014)
Kate E. Pickett and Richard G. Wilkinson 'Income in equality and health: A casual review', *Social Science & Medecine* 128: 316–26 (2015)

18

KATE PICKETT ON THE CASE FOR EQUALITY

Kate Pickett is Professor of Epidemiology in the Department of Health Sciences at the University of York. She is co-author, with Richard Wilkinson, of the bestselling *The Spirit Level*, winner of the 2012 Publication of the Year from the Political Studies Association and translated into 24 languages. Kate is also a co-founder and Trustee of the Equality Trust.

David Edmonds: *There are huge inequalities in the US between rich and poor. Some claim that this is one of the secrets to the dynamism of the US economy. There are tremendous rewards to be had from success: big homes, exotic holidays. Well, yes and no. Kate Pickett, of the University of York, is one half of the duo who wrote* The Spirit Level. *She says that in an unequal society, even the wealthy suffer.*

Nigel Warburton: *The topic we're focusing on is the case for equality. Could you begin by saying what kind of equality you're interested in?*

Kate Pickett: Our research focuses on social inequality, and by that I mean the vertical inequalities in society – how a society is structured hierarchically – and we use income inequality as a measure of that. Of course, there are all kinds of different inequalities that we don't focus on: for example, inequalities of ethnicity, of age, or of gender.

NW: *Are you saying that distribution of income is a measure of social hierarchy, or that it* is *the social hierarchy?*

KP: Both. Income inequality is easy to measure these days, so it's a useful way to compare different societies. But because we use our income in very social ways, because income has a social meaning, it turns out to be a really good measure of the social distances between us.

NW: *And we're talking about income, rather than wealth?*

KP: Yes, I'm sure wealth disparities work in the same way, but the data for income inequality is very good, and so that's the measure we use to compare different societies.

NW: *Could you say a bit about what kind of data you've gathered?*

KP: Well, I haven't gathered any of it. What we do is use data that other people have collected. We're always looking for robust measures that are internationally recognised as being comparable and reliable. So our income inequality data come from the United Nations Human Development reports, for example, and we use data on health from the World Health Organization.

NW: *And, globally, you found really interesting patterns about what inequality of income correlates with?*

KP: It's not quite global. We focus on the rich, developed market democracies, and there's a reason for that. For developing or emerging economies, the early stages of economic growth with rising standards of living are really important. The well-being of people in those societies depends on them having sufficient food, shelter, warmth etc. These societies need economic growth and for their living standards to go up. But in the rich, developed countries, there's no longer any relationship between a country getting richer and its health improving, or its happiness improving, or its well-being improving. It's as if we've got to the end of what economic growth can do for us in improving our societies. And so, over decades, you see countries getting richer and richer, but no improvement in their relative health or well-being. So what becomes important in a society like ours is relative social position, and that has a more powerful effect on our health and well-being than the fact that perhaps a very few of us may no longer have enough.

NW: *Is that a psychological effect? Are you saying that because I feel superior, in various ways, to people who earn less than me, I flourish? That seems odd?*

KP: Actually, I wouldn't call it just a psychological effect, more of a psycho-social effect. It's not just about how you feel in relation to others – both those above you and those below you in the structure of society – but also how those feelings affect your physiology. We know that low social status has a profound effect on chronic stress, for instance, which then can have profound effects on our health. But status can also affect the way we behave, both towards those above us and those below. So there is an emotional, psychological component to how you feel about your relative social status, but there are also these deep biological effects as well.

NW: *These effects are apparent on the people of relatively low social status. Are they apparent on the higher-status individuals?*

KP: There aren't that many studies that allow us to look at that; you need to be able to compare people at the same socio-economic position, across different societies. But from the studies we have, it's clear that the effect of inequality is most profound on the poorest, and the lowest social status, but it goes all the way up to the top. If you, with your level of education, or income, or your social class, were living in a more unequal society, you and your children would be more likely to have health and social problems than your counterparts living in a more equal place. We're comparing modern market democracies that are all capitalist societies, but there are striking differences in inequality between them. If you look at countries like Japan, Sweden, Norway, and Denmark, their income inequality, with the measure we use, is about twice that of, say, the UK, Australia, New Zealand, and the USA. So we're not talking about a difference between perfect equality and something horrendous. We don't have a society that has perfect equality. But we can see that societies that are a little bit more equal than us, or a fair bit more equal than us, or quite a lot more equal than us, do a lot better.

NW: *So are you really saying that if there's an incredibly wealthy individual in the USA, that person would be better off, in terms of health and happiness, if he or she moved to Japan or to one of the countries that has less inequality?*

KP: Yes. The data we have on income inequality doesn't include the super-rich. They're not there in surveys of income distribution. But if you're in the top, say, 20% of the income distribution, or the top 10% in some studies, or the top 5%, the benefits of greater equality extend up to you. So, yes, if you were that wealthy individual, in a more equal society, your life expectancy would, on average, be longer. Your children would be less likely to drop out of school, or do drugs, or become pregnant. You would be less likely to be a victim of crime. There are still problems that arise from living in a more unequal society, from which rich people cannot isolate themselves. So inequality is very destructive of the social fabric, the cohesion of society. You get more violence in a more unequal society, and we see a reaction to that among the rich with more gated communities, which is a fearful way to live. And if you live in a very unequal society where status matters so much more, there's a constant striving to keep up. That's a source of stress in itself. So, there are lots of ways in which inequality causes problems even for those who are achieving well.

NW: *Given that relative status is so important, mightn't there be a different way of changing people's attitude to status? Currently status is connected with wealth and income; but could we not find other markers of status, and so not get into difficulties associated with redistribution?*

KP: I'm interested to know what you think those markers might be.

NW: *Success in non-economic terms. Lots of people choose to be academics not for the money, certainly, but for the prestige that goes with being a respected scientist or expert on literature.*

KP: I think it's true that a lot of people find fulfilment through things other than income. But when we say 'a lot of people', it's quite clear that income is actually driving a lot of people's thoughts and perceptions and sense of well-being. Those who choose to 'opt out' of that rat race are rather unusual in society. A more equal society seems to give more people an opportunity to flourish and find value in the kinds of work they do, so that money is not the only marker of status.

NW: *Your research conclusions are potentially very interesting politically, because as a social scientist you're not just describing the world: you seem to be revealing implications that suggest we ought to change it.*

KP: That's true, and it's quite difficult as an academic social scientist to know where the boundaries of your discipline lie, and what your role should be in disseminating information that you have. We and others have built up a huge body of evidence on the damaging consequences of inequality, which have enormous political implications. Should one strive for growth, or should one strive for a fairer distribution of the proceeds of growth? I'm a social epidemiologist, so I see my job as trying to describe and understand the social causes of poor health and well-being. But I'm not a policy expert, so although my work has huge policy implications, I don't see it as my role to prescribe the policy solutions that would flow from that. However, the great thing we've also learned from our empirical research is that there are different ways that a society can become more equal. In Japan the income distribution is quite narrow to start with – there aren't huge pay ratios within Japan. In Sweden, which is about as equal as Japan, there are quite large income differences to start with, and it achieves its greater equality through taxation and redistribution. So it clearly doesn't matter too much how you get that greater equality; it just matters that you achieve it. That means there is a menu of policy options for people to think about.

NW: *You have to tease out causes and effects and distinguish them from mere correlations. But societies are so complex and so different. Japan is, in many respects, nothing like a Scandinavian country – so comparing them must be incredibly difficult.*

KP: Well, no, actually that makes it easier. Because if all the equal countries were all the same in some other way, all had exactly the same kind of welfare system, and all the unequal countries were different on that same factor, all had very contrasting welfare systems, then we might not be able to distinguish whether or not problems were caused by the welfare regime or by income inequality. So that heterogeneity, that variance in how countries achieve equality, is helpful in making the causal inference. And, of course, we would never say that inequalities are the only cause of the health and social problems we looked at. If we take, say, teenage births or homicides, clearly lots of different factors affect their prevalence in different societies. What we are saying is that inequality looks to be a common root cause across different societies of a whole range of problems.

NW: *Was that a discovery that you expected?*

KP: Well, we'd been working on health inequalities for a long time, and there's now a huge literature on income inequality and health. Separately, criminologists have long been looking at income inequality as a cause of violent crime. Once we started thinking about the psycho-social pathways, which lead from inequality to poor health, it became clear that we ought to see other behavioural or social consequences of inequality. Once we started looking at those, then there was a surprise that the picture was so consistent and the differences were so large. There is a ten- to sixteen-fold difference in imprisonment rates between different societies, a six-fold difference in teenage birth rates, a three- or four-fold difference in mental illness. So the range of things that seemed to be affected was striking, but we started looking across the range because of the strong picture that was already there for health.

NW: *So, how do you guard against the confirmation bias, the idea that if you look for a particular correlation you probably will find it, because you dismiss counter-evidence?*

KP: Obviously one tries not to do that. We were systematic in the selection of the countries we decided to look at from a list of the richest countries, excluding tax havens. We chose to look at health and social problems that have a strong social gradient and we chose to look at those that had good quality data. We decided that if we had a data source like the WHO, which provided data on the countries we had chosen to look at, we would take all of the data, and not just drop pieces of it. And we described cases where we found that what we were expecting didn't happen. There is, for instance, no relationship between income inequality and higher suicide rates. In fact, it goes in the opposite direction; more equal societies tend to have higher suicide rates. We think that is also to do with psycho-social effects on society, and whether or not you tend to blame yourself or society at large for your problems. There's no relationship between smoking and income inequality among adults, although recently someone has published a study showing that for young people there is. That is probably because all of the countries we look at are at very different points on the smoking epidemic.

The other surprising discovery was children's aspirations; it appeared that they were lower in more equal societies. It took a while to think about that, and then I realised that the societies where people were expressing higher aspirations were actually the ones with lower educational attainment. This is a very sad fact. I think what that is telling us is that the societies in which a lot of kids drop out of school or don't achieve their potential, are the unequal ones where money and status have become very important. Their aspirations are there, even though their capability of achieving them is not.

So we're always honest about finding relationships that don't fit the picture, and then trying to think about what explanations there might be for that. But we also subjected our inference to a couple of tests. We chose somebody else's index of well-being, the UNICEF index of child well-being, which has 40 different components in it, strongly related to inequality. And then we also decided to look at the 50 US states as a completely separate test, and found that for all of the things we're looking at, the relationship with inequality is there in the states as well.

NW: *I know that your work has been picked up by politicians, in Britain particularly, on both sides of the House. How do you feel about that?*

KP: I feel it's an excellent first step. The first step in changing whether or not we are a more equal society is for there to be a political debate about whether that is desirable, what the evidence tells us, and discussion about the policies we need to get there. I think the evidence is so convincing that whether you're on the political right, or the left, you ought to be thinking about solutions that make society more equal which are acceptable to your political ideology. And we have seen a real shift in the public debate around inequality, and in time, hopefully, we will see the policy shifts that help to achieve change. But it's not just been in the UK that our work has been of interest. It's been debated in parliaments in New Zealand, in Canada, and in other places as well. And we work with an international group, the Alliance for Sustainability and Prosperity, to influence bodies such as the United Nations to think about development in new ways. This is about creating sustainable development that maximises well-being. That requires working with people from lots of different disciplines. Not only are social epidemiologists showing the appalling consequences of inequality for health and well-being; economists are now starting to look very closely at inequality as a cause of economic instability. So that's important, because it adds a range of evidence that helps make the case for greater equality.

NW: *You've had critics as well as supporters, and some of them have been quite vocal. Have any of them come up with serious evidence that made you think again?*

KP: No. I think that most of the criticisms were ill-informed and shallow, and that actually the body of evidence that exists is really solid. Since we published our book, research on inequality has expanded and there's a flood of new research that is constantly coming across our desks showing that inequality is related to things we hadn't thought of, or confirming some of our hunches. So no, I don't feel that there has been any serious criticism that we can't answer or address, or that makes us feel shaky about the evidence that is there.

FURTHER READING

Richard Wilkinson and Kate Pickett, *The Spirit Level* (Penguin, 2010)
Roberto de Vogli, *Progress or Collapse: The Crises of Market Greed* (Routledge, 2013)
Danny Dorling, *Inequality and the 1%* (Verso, 2014)

Lightning Source UK Ltd.
Milton Keynes UK
UKHW050004040223
416413UK00020B/2023

9 781473 913806